The Creative Edge

The Creative Edge

INSPIRING ART EXPLORATIONS IN LIBRARIES AND BEYOND

Mary C. Fletcher

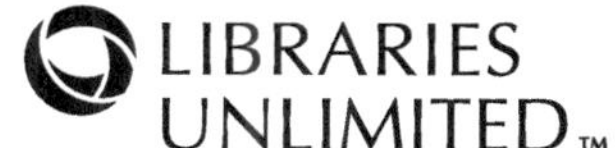

LIBRARIES UNLIMITED™

An Imprint of ABC-CLIO, LLC

Santa Barbara, California • Denver, Colorado

Library of Congress Cataloging in Publication Control Number: 2019008336

ISBN: 978-1-4408-6109-3 (paperback)
     978-1-4408-6110-9 (ebook)

23 22 21 20 19   1 2 3 4 5

This book is also available as an eBook.

Libraries Unlimited
An Imprint of ABC-CLIO, LLC

ABC-CLIO, LLC
147 Castilian Drive
Santa Barbara, California 93117
www.abc-clio.com

This book is printed on acid-free paper ∞

Manufactured in the United States of America

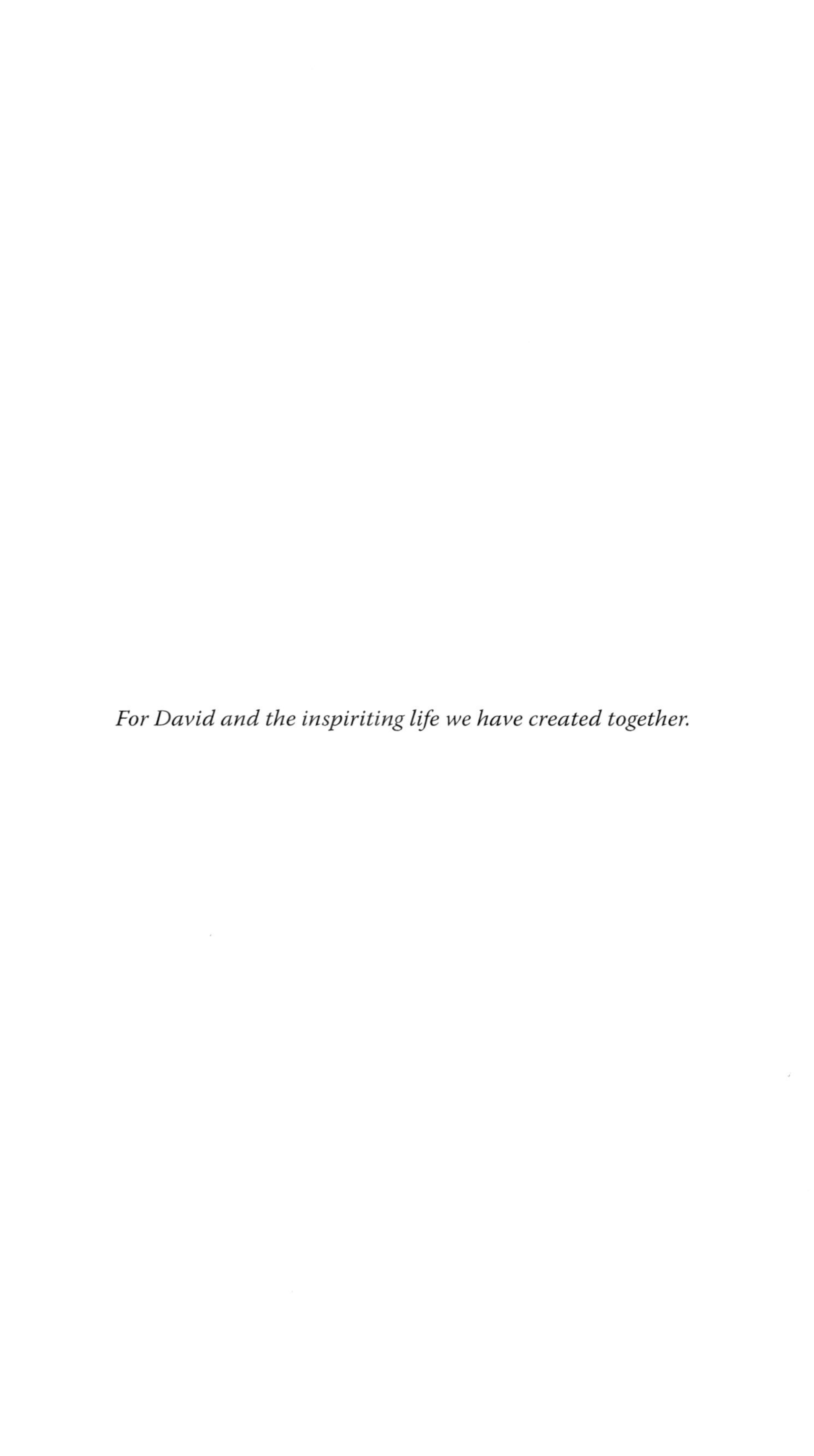

For David and the inspiriting life we have created together.

Contents

Acknowledgments

I am deeply grateful to the artists of all ages who have attended these creativity programs, with special thanks to those who have kindly consented to contribute their photo images and artwork to this book.

I wish to express my profound gratitude to all those at the Avon Free Public Library. Foremost, I am deeply grateful to Kari Ann St. Jean, Children's and Teen Services Manager, and Glenn Grube, Library Director, for having the vision to create an art studio in a public library. Thank you for taking up the carpet and putting down the tiles! Thank you for believing that creativity programming belongs in libraries.

I wish to extend my special thanks to Megan Grosch and April Jones for years of dedicated work as intuitive and insightful facilitators of creativity. Thank you to Marisa Hicking for enthusiastically inspiring teens to express their creativity. I am grateful to everyone at the Avon Free Public Library. Those who have contributed their expertise and support to these creativity programs include Catherine Cavanaugh, Jack Clonan, Levin Cusatis, Rachel Cutler, Jaimee Eldred, Barbara Greenleaf, Holly Greer, Tabbi Heavner, Suzanne Lancaster, Cynthia Larsen, Elise Montes, Jessica Noble, Wanda Oprica, Leona Mae Page, Tina Panik, Susan Reboul, Jeanna Shillington, Becca Shillington, Amanda Stern, Marisa Tassinari, Rhoda Valentine, Patricia Valsecchi, Jennifer Wilson, and so many more! Thank you to all others who have given their ideas, time, and energy to support library creativity programs. Thank you to Lisa Berman for all she has reclaimed for the art studio. Special thanks is given to Peter Anderson for his keen interest and uplifting humor during the long process of writing this book.

Thank you to members of Library Board and Friends of the Avon Free Public Library and the Simsbury Public Library. Thank you to all who have donated funds and supplies so that creative programs can continue to be offered in libraries.

I am grateful to Chelesea Jenkins for her valuable help in facilitating and sustaining the art program at the Simsbury Library, with special thanks to Lisa Karim, Stephanie Prato, and Hilary Kennard. Thank you also to Jan Madrak and Cheryl Donahue for your love of art and establishing the foundation for creativity programs at the library. Thank you to Jessica Archambault, Erica Hsia, Sara Ray, Pam Sikora, Mara Whitman, and all of the current and former employees who contributed to the development of creativity programs at the Simsbury Public Library. A very special thanks to Gina Morgan for generously donating her time and expertise to reading and correcting these pages.

Deepest thanks to my editor, Jessica Gribble, for all her knowledge, cheerful reassurance, encouragement, and patience with my creative process. I am grateful to Eswari Maruthu and all who have dedicated their valuable services to copyedit this book.

Thanks to the staff of the Art Studio at the Eric Carle Museum of Picture Book Art, especially to Meghan Burch for mentoring the initial establishment of our art studio room.

I am indebted to MaryAnn Kohl and Susan Striker for the inspiration of their books. Thank you for their guidance and encouragement in writing a book of my own.

I wish to express my gratitude to Miguel A. Figueroa, Director of the Center for the Future of Libraries, and Paula Holmes from the Association for Library Service to Children for their support. Thank you to Disney for sponsoring the ALSC Curiosity Creates Grant envisioning creativity programming as a new direction for libraries!

Thank you to Hervé Tullet for inspiring us all! Thank you to Eric Lehman, Amy Nawrocki, Cheryl Mowry, Colleen Akiko, and Mary and Fred Fletcher for their friendship and wisdom.

I am most grateful to my dear husband, David K. Leff, for his abiding love, caring support, and creative guidance. Thank you to Ariel Prechtl, Josh Leff, and Tiki Diliberto for the inspiration of their creative spirit!

Introduction

INSPIRING LIBRARIES

Libraries can go beyond being sources for information and become sources for inspiration. The intention of this book is to enable libraries to become centers of creativity. These programs and offerings should not be limited to the visual arts, but inclusive of all the arts: creative writing, drama, music, and dance. Creativity extends far beyond the arts into the realms of science, technology, business, politics and more. Creativity is interwoven into everyday experience. To some extent, libraries have always been places of inspiration. But it is time to recognize the significance of this service and to intentionally do more. It is time to balance technology with creativity and to balance information with inspiration.

Libraries can set the standard for offering creativity programs with the unique potential to reach everyone in the community, regardless of age or socioeconomic background. If this is to happen, library science students will need to be offered the opportunity to become specialists in creativity, as well as specialists in information and technology. This will greatly extend and deepen the quality of services libraries can provide, changing the very definition of what a library can be. Recognized as a center for the arts in the community, a library could not only be a place to view art on a gallery wall but also a place to create works of art. Also, it can not only be a place to listen to author lectures but also a place that inspires original stories to be written, illustrated, and acted out through programming for creativity.

Libraries can go beyond being places to listen to musical performances and also be places to take an active part in singing, playing instruments, and composing music. Community rooms can hold both dance performances and celebrate family dance nights. Libraries can go beyond having art galleries to having creative art studios.

Children can do much more than just sit quietly during storytime and then paste a precut craft. When storytime evolves into an active and interactive experience, children are encouraged to explore, express, and create. They can go beyond words and into the meaning of the art in a picture book. They can interpret and embody the elements of stories through inventing yoga poses. Children can imaginatively "be" birds and trees and the wind. They can rejoice in dancing, singing, and performing their own ideas and in creating original art during storytime.

Future librarians need not be known for shushing everyone down into silence. Instead, they can be known for opening up creative expression by saying, "Tell me more! Show me your ideas!"

BEYOND SURFACES

This book goes beyond surfaces. The emphasis is not on making art products, but on the value of the creative process. Rather than offer a series of step-by-step projects to copy, open-ended art ideas are offered. These simple ideas were inspired by many sources and have been gathered here to pass along to you and for you to pass them on to others.

This book is primarily about making art with children in libraries, but the ideas are not limited to working with children and are certainly not limited to working within library walls. The ideas extend far beyond these confines. Just about anyone . . . anywhere . . . anytime can decide to take the journey into open art. Since it is about exploration, the destination will indeed be all along the way.

Creativity-based art programs can be offered for children in day-care centers, nursery schools, preschools, or as afterschool programs. Open art studio areas can be set in recreation facilities or senior centers, as well as rehabilitation centers and hospitals. Art centers and museums are ideal places to offer open art experiences for all ages.

Open-ended art experiences encourage choices and expand possibilities. This book is not about making crafts, teaching art, or providing art therapy services. It is about the creative process. Experts on creativity speak about "facilitating" the art process rather than directing the way. Inspiring art materials and themes provide a course of action for creativity. Cooperative works, such as murals, offer overarching ideas with guidelines that open up possibilities. The whole truly becomes greater than the sum of its parts in a collaborative work of art.

Libraries can have both makerspaces and creative places. We can teach how to make products using tools and technology in a makerspace and also facilitate art in a creative place. Ultimately, the goal of art-based creativity programs will be to enable participants to explore their own creative direction. For each one working in an art group, it is a solitary experience that takes place in a public setting—people working independently together. Because the emphasis is on the art process, participants explore their own ideas and encounter their own self-directed discoveries along the way.

A FACILITATOR OF CREATIVITY

Where does one begin to learn how to facilitate creativity? Start by taking the invitation that you will offer others. On your own, become acquainted with the art explorations and experiences in this book. Start anywhere, and go forward. Become immersed in the process. Find your own way. Direct your own choices. Learn the potential and limitations of each medium. Take chances, combine art materials. Mixing media can open up an astounding array of possibilities. Find out what happens if . . .

A facilitator of the creative process does not give step-by-step instructions to follow. It may seem to be a paradox that a facilitator must first learn *not* to teach. But the aim is to provide an environment for art making that is free from directives, critical analysis, restrictive standards, or competitive grading systems. Because creative choices are valued, there will be a wide variety of unique and imaginative responses to the art materials. As art explorations occur, the process can become deeply engaging and full of surprising discoveries.

Creativity facilitators are attentive, but at a respectful distance. When help is needed, a facilitator will respond in a way that supports the decision-making abilities of the individual. This means being a supportive guide on the side to assist the search for alternatives and possibilities, but not pointing out a single solution. This open-ended and nonjudgmental approach respects individual choices, problem-solving skills, and autonomy. There is a Zen-like quality to this nondirective approach, and the words of the *Tao Te Ching* have been interspersed throughout this text.

> The journey of a thousand miles starts from beneath your feet.
>
> —Lao Tzu, *Tao Te Ching,* Chapter 64

It is hoped that the eventual outcome will bring the opportunity for specialization in creativity through the universities that educate librarians.

THE GIFT THAT KEEPS ON GIVING

The focus of this book is on the visual arts, but this is only one aspect of the multifaceted potential of creativity programming. Opportunities such as these are needed everywhere, especially in low-income communities where budget cuts have greatly reduced or eliminated the arts in education and the access to the arts in the community. As a result, this book focuses on the selection of art ideas that are simple to present, high in quality, low in cost, and open-ended for those who will receive them.

Creativity programs offer the ultimate gift that keeps on giving. So why are they not offered everywhere? The surprising truth is that most systems are biased *against* creativity. This book will examine the evidence of this negative bias, why it is, why it continues to exist, and what can be done about it. How, for instance, do we move toward creativity programming in a place where it has not existed before, or where it is considered a frivolous pastime? The answer is to prove the value, by speaking a language that can be understood by administrators. Arts-based creativity programs do not need to be expensive. They are cost effective. Creativity programs meet a need that is not available elsewhere. The value can be measured, both in program attendance and the quality of response.

Keeping an art program sustainable, however, means going beyond attendance statistics to also providing photo documentation and notes on both the creative process and product. This will be an irreplaceable resource and will provide evidence that documents the value of creativity programming. This book exists because of such documentation. An ongoing archive holds more than photos of final art products and will also include the ardent expressions and spirited hands of those involved in the creative process. Ultimately, these artists are the focus of our work, and when they exuberantly hold up their completed artwork for the camera, these are moments well worth keeping.

THE BIAS AGAINST CREATIVITY

There is, however, an undeniable bias against creativity. If we are utterly honest about it, it is within us all. It is much safer to not take creative risks. So it is inevitable that we will encounter others who challenge its worth. We will then be called upon to explain why it is important to value creativity and the negative consequences of not doing so. Trite answers and truisms will not do. Creativity is more than just fun and trendy. If such programming is to be developed and sustained with funding, it is important to give respectful and thoughtful responses based on scientific evidence and effective practices.

Most people, surprisingly, do not know much about creativity or have been misinformed through common myths. This makes it all the more essential that we keep well informed through delving into landmark studies as well as the most recent research and current practices. There are abundant resources in the findings of experts in the field of creativity. Learn from those who have led the way. Some will be mentioned in this book, and they will guide you to others.

First, we begin within ourselves. We must admit our own resistance to change before we can muster the courage to confront and overcome it. Only then can we learn how to tap into our own creative resources and find innovative solutions within the system around us. By choosing to read this book, you have already begun. Those who find the courage to act on their beliefs will be amazed at how many others are on their side. You are not alone.

1

The Arts and Creativity

ENVISION AND CREATE

Henry David Thoreau once defined a "truly good book" as one that inspires one to live it. He proclaimed, "What I began by reading I must finish by acting" (Thoreau 1971, 223).

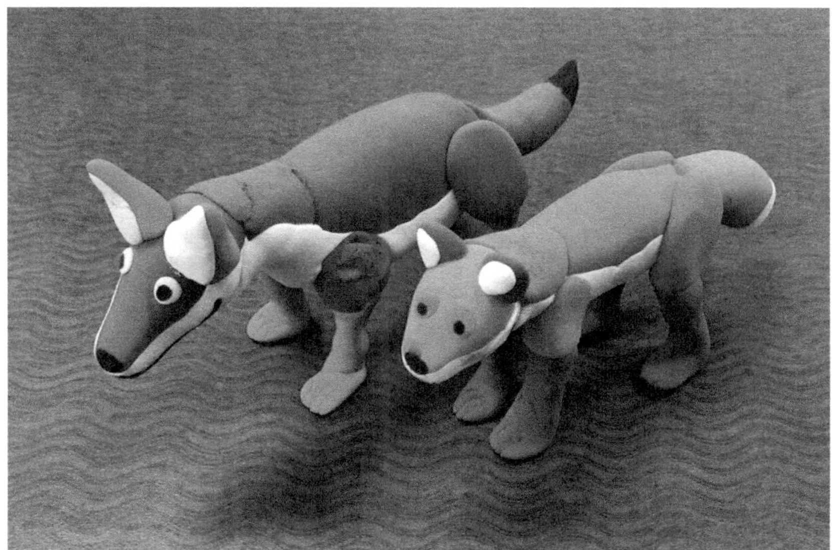

Figure 1.1 Artwork by Brian and Matthew Dunham.

The intention of this book is to inspire thoughts that lead to action. Before we begin, we must see what is missing, visualize how things can be, and then act to bring about this change. It is not enough just to see another way. Visionaries express to others what they see and enable others to envision it too. This is what artists do every day. This is what we can all do.

We are all creative beings, and most of us do not know this. Old beliefs and myths about creativity have obstructed our understanding. Scientific research has dispelled many of the misunderstandings that previously devalued creativity or placed it only in the exclusive realm of geniuses. These myths have been replaced by mounting scientific evidence that creativity is crucial to childhood development and to our development as a species. Nurturing creativity in young children and implementing programs that sustain creative growth throughout life can no longer be considered a "frill" but are increasingly being recognized as a necessity.

The Center for Childhood Creativity has issued a white paper, "Inspiring a Generation to Create: Critical Components of Creativity in Children," examining what skills or processes contribute to creativity in children and how to foster these skills. The findings were based on research in the fields of psychology, neuroscience, education, and business. The key components of creativity in children aged 6–14 years were identified as imagination and originality, flexibility, decision making, communication and self-expression, motivation, collaboration, action, and movement. All children have creative potential, and these skills can be enhanced in an environment that encourages creativity to flourish. "Creativity is not a fixed quantity, but rather a renewable resource that can be improved and nurtured by optimizing the environment that allows an individual's creative potential to blossom. . . . Children need time to immerse themselves in creative activities, a place that feels safe to express ideas that are unconventional, and encouragement to explore the unknown so they can discover what they enjoy and unlock a universe of possibilities" (Hadani and Jaeger 2015, 5).

At the Avon Free Public Library, Kari Ann St. Jean, Children's and Teen Services Manager, has found innovative ways to bring creativity into children's programming. By designing a series of sessions entitled "Stories in Motion," she has integrated yoga-based creative movement into storytime. She explains,

> As librarians, we are trained to present storytime using books, props, action rhymes, and fingerplays. Children are taught to follow our lead. I have experimented with this format by asking participants to *embody* the movement in stories and rhymes. For instance, instead of walking our fingers up the waterspout, we use our whole body to become spiders; we become the rain and sun; we all get 'washed out' and try again. Interpreting the rhyme becomes experiential and interactive. As we imaginatively become spiders, we awaken

our senses, emotions, and memories. We extend our nonverbal vocabularies and neurological connections. Instead of passively mimicking finger movements, we invent our *own* actions, and storytime is transformed! The presenter is no longer the solitary point of focus. Rather, everyone's creativity is central to the experience. The result is an interconnected experiential set of imaginative activities that only exist in the here and now. I must add that, in order to facilitate storytime this way, one must relish playfully bringing stories to life. One must have the courage to explore uncharted territory to change traditional ways. One must have the courage to trust oneself and to trust the creativity of children to guide the way.

With innovative programming such as this, 21st-century libraries can be at the forefront of meeting the creative needs of children and the community. Establishing this environment, however, will require a fundamental change in how the system views art and creativity if the myths continue to exist there. Most likely, they do. In this age of information, there is so much we do not understand. Strides may have been made, but there is a long way to go.

Few understand how children's art and literacy are fundamentally related. This correlation has been well documented but continues to be underestimated and misunderstood even by educators. Since babies and toddlers are brought to libraries long before they begin to attend preschool, libraries can offer programs that will address the developmental and creative needs of our youngest children.

It is possible to establish sustainable art-based creativity programs even in places where they have never existed before. This will involve learning how to plan and use intentional strategies that open the way for creativity while maintaining the ability to be spontaneous, flexible, and improvise. Inspired by existing art studios in children's museums that serve intergenerational groups, these programs strive to nurture and sustain creative development throughout life.

ART IN THE LIBRARY

This book centers on an art-based creativity program in Avon Free Public Library in Avon, Connecticut. Beginning many years ago as a children's art group, it is now thriving as ongoing creativity programming serving multiple generations that has received national attention.

Inspired by the Art Studio at the Boston Children's Museum and mentored by the Art Studio at the Eric Carle Museum of Picture Book Art, the Avon Free Public Library's existing creativity programs were expanded by establishing one of the first designated art studios located in a public library in the country.

Avon Library was chosen by the Association for Library Service to Children (ALSC) in 2015 to be one of the recipients of the ALSC Curiosity Creates Grant sponsored by Disney. The resulting library program, The Creative Edge, was based on the research from the Center for Childhood Creativity white paper entitled "Inspiring a Generation to Create: Critical Components of Creativity in Childhood." Avon's program was subsequently selected as one of the libraries representing the best practices. This resulted in an article published in 2016 in *Children and Libraries: The Journal of the Association for Library Services to Children*, entitled "On the Creative Edge: The Artistic Side of One Library." Written by Mary C. Fletcher, this article has provided the foundation for this book.

The Avon Free Public Library was selected to present at the Symposium on the Future of Libraries held in Atlanta, Georgia, in January 2017. That presentation, entitled "The Creative Edge: The Art of Creativity Programming in Libraries," contained an overview of ideas that have been further researched, expanded, and detailed for this publication.

This book describes how to design an innovative art program from the inside out. Sustaining art-based creativity programming, however, requires a deeper commitment than only a few "special" art sessions now and then. It requires long-term investment in quality art materials, and it is helpful to have a designated space that can be used on a regular basis for artmaking. Most importantly, administrations need to invest in staff by allowing for the time, training, and support necessary to establish and expand an ongoing art program. The programs based in the Art Studio have included Open Art Studio (all ages), Early Art (ages 2 and 3, with a caregiver), Story Art (grades 1–3), Creative Art (school-age children, grades 1–6), and Teen Art Programs.

This book provides an overview of ideas and approaches, rather than rigidly structured methods of procedure on how to conduct a specific group. Psychological studies and neuroscientific research will be cited that dispel myths about creativity. This book will lead you to explore other sources of information, some of which are listed in the references. The art experiences have been chosen for simplicity and open-ended possibilities. It is hoped that they will provide a starting point for your own explorations.

Mainly, the intention is to enable you to draw upon your own resources and those around you to bring about creative change. This is an invitation for you to enter the creative process, an enticement to adventure into realms where the destination is unknown. The exploratory process advances as an ever-changing mark moved by choices and unexpected findings along the way. It is always at the edge of our experience, pushing further on. The end purpose will be at every point. No one can lead your way. It is a self-guided journey, influenced by all that has come before and what can yet come to be. The creative edge is the brink of discovery.

SUSTAINING CREATIVITY PROGRAMS

It is possible to establish and sustain creativity programming in such places as libraries. When success is evaluated through statistics, creativity programs are proven winners. Based on these findings, high attendance rates are to be expected. More importantly, participants have provided enthusiastic evaluations of such programs.

Funding, however, will always be a basic issue. Learn the defined boundaries of the system where you work. Systems usually excel at establishing these parameters. Goals are set, and success is evaluated with numbers and statistics. Consider whether budgetary constraints have been used as an excuse to keep things the same, squeeze tight, and constrict innovation, or whether chances have been taken. How have new ideas been funded previously? Is there some flexibility in the language of the budget? What about grants? What about local patron donations? How was funding obtained in the past for innovative programming? What was the source, and what was the outcome?

Understanding a workplace such as a library means researching how funds have been prioritized for allocation. This will give insight into the values of the system. How can creativity programming become recognized as valuable, even a vital component, in such a system? There are many measures of this necessity. Compelling testimony comes from the findings of experts in science, psychology, education, and business that have determined the need to nurture creative minds in order to provide the foundation for successful, fulfilling, and self-actualized lives. Furthermore, creativity and innovation will be necessary to confront entrenched issues, expanding problems, and the increasing complexities of the coming years.

THINK OUTSIDE THE BOX WHILE WORKING WITHIN IT

Creative art programs in libraries can reach diverse groups of all ages and abilities. Creative art is not about teaching crafts. It is not an art education program. There are no examples to follow or techniques to copy. No lesson plans will be written to obtain and evaluate specific art objectives. Rather, the ideas are designed to be process-oriented and open-ended to invite exploration. Although the artwork takes place in a group, the direction of each response will be self-guided. What happens along the way will be a singular creative experience.

This may sound simple, but it is a radical departure from the past arts and crafts experiences of the participants. Most often, arts and crafts require following step-by-step directions to copy a specific product. Programs featuring crafts have traditionally been held in libraries, camps, or after school, or even during school, as part of art education. Crafts can teach useful skills, but these assembly-type experiences are not to be confused with creativity programming.

Most of us were taught art in an elementary class where our work was judged, compared to others, critiqued, and graded. The creative choices in many of these art classes were extremely limited. Art products were evaluated by the degree of skill demonstrated in following the directives of the lesson, such as learning one-point perspective or drawing detailed and realistic representations. Such an art educational approach is instructive, but, as a result, many learned they were not artistic or creative. As adults, these beliefs were passed on to their children.

Artistic or creative work has usually not been regarded as a serious academic pursuit. Part of the ongoing problem is that our educational system still tends to mostly confine creativity to the arts. Since the arts are usually segregated from "serious" academic studies, creativity has been marginalized too. This lack of understanding about creativity and the persistence of myths about artists have been noted by many studies written by creativity researchers. Artists and creatives are seen as unreachable stars or unapproachable outsiders "way out there" on the fringes of society.

Research, however, has documented how essential creativity and the arts are for child development. Art education can best be approached through methods that respect and enhance creative confidence and abilities. Art-based creativity programs in libraries can be used to supplement but can never replace a quality art education.

Advocates are needed to keep quality art education deeply embedded in the schools, especially during difficult times when it is continuously under threat of elimination. Furthermore, excellent teachers are needed throughout the educational system who understand how to incorporate the arts across the curriculum. Ironically, the threat to funding continues despite mounting evidence of the critical importance of the arts, creativity, and choice-based initiatives for the development of 21st-century skills.

Open art experiences in libraries can offer progressive methods of presenting art that are conducive to creative development. Furthermore, these experiences would be inclusive of all ages, encompass many styles of learning, and welcoming for individuals with all levels of abilities.

MAKERSPACES AND CREATIVE PLACES

Makerspace areas for younger children encourage hands-on play. Children can build with wooden blocks, manipulate bright shapes on light tables, connect magnets, and interconnect toy pieces in myriad ways. These engaging experiences develop motor skills, hand-eye coordination, balance, shape, and color recognition. Best of all, this happens while having the fun of making and unmaking, constructing and deconstructing. It is mostly about the process, and the product is meant to come undone. Just knock the tower down! The undoing can be the most fun of all!

Many libraries with these constructing areas are also striving to offer labs and makerspaces that meet the needs of all ages while keeping pace with advances in technology. Starting with young children, many libraries are offering opportunities to gain experience in coding and robotics. Consistent with the goal to keep up with the latest advances, makerspaces designed for older children, teens, and adults emphasize product making, primarily through the use of technology: 3-D printers, digital sewing and embroidery machines, electronic die-cutting machines, tablets for creating digital art, and an array of electronic devices and tools for the maker. For the most part, however, the machines actually make the products: 3-D printed plastic objects, embroidered designs, die-cut shapes, and computer-generated imagery. Learning how to program and guide these devices certainly extends our abilities to make things faster and with precision. Through technology, the quality of products can be improved, and, doubtlessly, the quantity of production is vastly increased.

Makerspaces have also been extended to provide hands-on experiences such as coloring, doodling, calligraphy, origami, and folded book art. There are groups for jewelry making, knitting, hand sewing, embroidery, weaving, and countless other enjoyable activities teaching valuable skills. Yet, to the degree that the products result directly from patterns and templates, they are not creative. The abilities being acquired, however, have the potential to be developed into designing original creations.

Many people are using makerspaces to experiment with ideas and create art. Some libraries have invested in digital whiteboards, interactive projectors, movie-making equipment, and virtual reality devices that can open up new realms for creative minds. We can only glimpse the future possibilities as makerspaces increasingly become the venue for creativity and innovation.

Architects now design libraries and renovations to plan for makerspaces, and they have been rightly incorporated into our vision of what libraries can be. The next step is to provide places for art and other creative experiences, starting with the youngest children.

During an art experience, hands and eyes direct the process all along the way. There is no preprogrammed outcome reached following templates and patterns, or by tapping keys and touching screens. Creative experiences are often evolving ideas, forming and reforming, imperfect and incomplete. It is less about *making* something and more about *experiencing* something—an unfolding process. It is the slightest touch that changes the clay. It is the stickiness of the glue that holds together pieces of an idea. It is the lush line of paint and the frustrating drip run that becomes the inspiration to change the painted horse into a giraffe.

Since with young children the creative process is exploratory, there is no preset direct route to a destination. It is not the express lane on the highway. Creative exploration is more like a visual excursion on a winding road with many secondary avenues and diversions all along the way. One decision leads to another. Since it is a self-guided exploration, with curiosity leading the way, the route will be subject to change and open to unexpected turns. What began with one idea may end up as something entirely different. However, it will not be someone else's idea of where to go. It will be infused with personal meaning and imagination. It will be a unique experience that can lead to unprecedented finds and expansive discoveries. This is art.

Albert Einstein once remarked in an interview, "I am enough of the artist to draw freely upon my imagination. Imagination is more important than knowledge. Knowledge is limited. Imagination encircles the world" (Viereck 1929, 117).

WHAT DOES ART HAVE TO DO WITH LITERACY?

There is a profound connection between art and literacy that merits attention from the beginning. The National Association for the Education of Young Children (NAEYC) and the International Reading Association (IRA) have issued a joint position statement entitled "Learning to Read and Write: Developmentally Appropriate Practices for Young Children." Important experiences are recommended during the infant and toddler years to "lay the foundation for later literacy learning." These recommendations included "providing simple art materials such as crayons, markers, and large paper for toddlers to explore and manipulate" (NAEYC/IRA 1998, 9).

Educator and researcher Rhoda Kellogg contends, "The opportunity to scribble freely has meaning for two critical operations of intelligence: reading and writing. Scribbling promotes the hand-eye coordination needed for writing." She adds, "In learning to read, the child must perceive line formations that are like the ones he has made spontaneously" (Kellogg 2015, 262). Early art experiences are the building blocks of both art and written language. The child will spontaneously make circles; dots; loops; curves; horizontal, diagonal, and vertical lines; and more. No one needs to teach this to the child. Yet these 20 basic scribble components form the basis for every written language symbol in the world!

To support early spontaneous art is to support the foundations of literacy. Yet this is not widely known. Scribbling is still considered a waste of paper by many parents, childcare providers, and even early educators. Children's artwork is not taken seriously despite what psychologists and other researchers have determined to be the crucial value of art and creative experiences in childhood. Libraries can move to the forefront to become places where art and creativity are nurtured and recognized as essential to child development and literacy.

Howard Gardner, renowned for his theory of multiple intelligences, wrote in depth about the significance of children's artwork in his book *Artful Scribbles*. He maintained, "The drawings of young schoolchildren are often their most striking creations: vibrant, expressive, exhibiting a strong command of form and considerable beauty." Moreover, this art evolves in a sequence that is self-taught. Gardner continues, "No one shows the child how to do this—and, equally amazing, each normal child, progressing at his own rate, seems to go through just this sequence. By now we would consider it a sign of ignorance, if not gross neglect, to disregard these products of our children's hands" (Gardner 1980, 5–6).

THE ARTS AND CREATIVITY IN SCHOOLS

Given the urgency to develop creative minds, the question arises: Are the schools providing creativity programming? For the most part, the answer is no. Despite the ever-mounting evidence supporting the need for the arts and creativity programs, they have been historically underestimated, undervalued, and even undermined. This is why it is very important to advocate for programs that foster art and creativity.

Recently there has been momentum in this direction, as evidenced by STEM (Science, Technology, Engineering, Math) to STEAM (which inserts the "A" for Arts). These initiatives seek to incorporate the arts into the teaching of the science, technology, engineering, and math. Correspondingly, the teaching of art influenced by STEM objectives will be inspirational to the next generation of inventors and innovators.

There is also a trend toward openness in art education in some systems as evidenced by choice-based movements such as the Open Art Room and TAB (Teaching for Artistic Behavior). Many educators admit there is a long way to go before creativity can be incorporated—*even into art education*. Unfortunately, with increasing demands toward standardization, time and money continue to be diverted to meet these ends. The arts will likely remain vulnerable to being sliced first when cuts are made. The arts in our schools will continue to be in peril, if they manage to survive at all. It is impossible to calculate how immense the long-term damage of these losses will be. How will we ever be able to measure what might have been?

CREATIVITY IN LIBRARIES

Places such as libraries can set the standard for quality creativity programming that is free of the restriction to "teach to the test." Moreover, libraries are free from the educational requirements to teach—at all. There are no tasks to direct and no evaluation of how well the lesson plan has been followed. There are no grades, no bell curve. There is no teacher, no students. There is a creativity facilitator and an invitation to create. This opens the possibilities for individuals to fully engage in creative endeavors that lead to deeper self-guided learning experiences. Libraries are the ideal setting for such opportunities. Creativity can thrive there.

Many would assert that libraries have already recognized this need and have made significant progress in this direction by citing the installation of makerspaces and other programs that have creative components. Surely progress has been made, but the commitment to creativity must be deepened and widened. It is necessary to become more inclusive and continuous, reaching more people more of the time, especially impoverished communities with little or no access to the arts through the education system. It is essential to develop programs that promote curiosity, exploration, experimentation, expression, and imagination. These programs can model creativity by being flexible, open-ended, and playful, while encouraging individualism, original thinking, and imagination.

Creative art studios can be a valuable asset in libraries. Those who are motivated to be part of such a change are now challenged to become more informed through researching creativity and learning how to facilitate the creative process. To become one who specializes in facilitating creativity is to embark on a fascinating journey of discovery—about oneself and others. We are capable of far more than we have been led to believe. We *are* creative beings.

This is a book that will go beyond "how to" to answer a much more important question: Why. Why is creativity so important and why has its value been so underestimated? What is the bias against creativity? Research has established that we are all born with creative potential. How can it be that we do not know this? Why do most of us perceive ourselves as *not* creative? How can we move beyond these misconceptions that so limit our potential and the potential of our children? Given all there is to gain, this book ultimately asks the question: Why not try?

2

The Creative Edge

THE EDGE

The creative edge is a vantage point for insight, inspiration, and imagination. It is the ability to see what is missing and to go beyond previous limitations. It is a competition with self, not with others. It is to look forward, anticipate the unexpected, and thrive on the challenge of change.

The approach to the creative edge is unmarked. It is reached through the willingness to take risks, admit missteps, and persevere despite setbacks to discover our own way. When we are at the limit of our proven abilities, we are on the creative edge. With a sense of wonder and awe at possibilities, it is risking the adventure beyond into an unknown realm. When we dare to venture past this edge, the boundary line moves with us. This is the growing edge that will expand us. It will widen our experience and increase our capacities. Through this encounter, we are becoming more than we were before. This is the creative edge.

THE ORIGINS OF THE OPEN ART STUDIO

The Avon Free Public Library in Connecticut has established one of the first art studios in a public library in the country. As a place designated for creativity in the children's department, the art studio was differentiated from conventional arts and crafts rooms or makerspaces. The philosophy of offering process-oriented and open-ended art experiences led to the naming of the Open Art Studio program that would welcome individuals of all ages and levels of ability.

We have learned from our experiences that open art in a library unites generations and brings the community together. Art bridges all ages and spans great distances. Often, three generations of the same family create artwork side by side. We have seen patrons from China, Korea, Russia, Eastern Europe, and South America working together. Originating from around the world, first-generation immigrants and their families, who now reside in surrounding communities, meet at the library to share the universal language of art (Fletcher 2016, 11). This is a place to come together. Although there are cultural differences, language differences, and age differences, through the language of art there is understanding. Art is thought made visible. It is more than expression; it is communication.

BEYOND ASSEMBLY CRAFT

When we first began to address the need to design and implement art-based creativity programs, some responded by saying that we already have creativity in libraries. We have all sorts of arts and crafts programs, and we always have crafts after storytime! But, upon close examination, most "arts and crafts" activities actually have very little to do with either art or creativity. An experience that requires following directions to put pieces together in one "correct" way is more similar to factory assembly work than artwork. It is definitely not creative. Learning assembly tasks was important for work in centuries past, but these methods do not support the development of creativity and innovation necessary in the 21st century.

When there are no chances for choice, there is no possibility for originality—and it is *not* a creative art experience. If much of what has been commonly promoted as art or creativity programming is actually not, then there is much less of this programming than we have been led to believe. It is not that it does not exist, but it is relatively rare.

This leads us to think twice about "art and crafts activities" in which the objective is to make cute, clever, bedazzled, and adorable products fashioned from adult ideas of what children "should" do in their spare time. Many adults remember arts and crafts from long ago in camp or in library programs—even in art class at school. Toilet-paper-roll caterpillars, leprechaun hats, cotton-ball-tailed bunnies, egg-carton spiders, and googly-eyed reindeer clothespins all come from adult ideas of cuteness. When children are required to follow adult instructions step-by-step to make look-alike products, these experiences close the door to creative responses.

Children are also required to make "beautiful" products according to adult standards when given a recipe to follow for an attractive end product:

"Let's all paint gorgeous sunsets using red and yellow!" In this instance, once again, there is little chance for creativity. If the resulting products all look the same (or strikingly similar), then the process may have been instructive but has not been creative. Adults working with children need to be careful not to shut out creative responses in the pursuit of beauty.

The creative process does not necessarily result in a beautiful product. In fact, it often does not. This is one of the many reasons why it is so worthwhile. Freed from the necessity to please others, children can satisfy their own curiosity by pursuing their own ideas, joys, and interests. The work they will do will be authentically their own and meaningful for them. This happens when the door is kept open to experimentation, self-guided exploration, and the wondrous joy of discovery.

The resulting products will probably not be art show quality according to adult standards, and this is how it should be. *Making* something is overemphasized by adults. Everything has to be something or stand for something else. "What are you making?" is a frequent question adult caregivers ask children who are enjoying experimenting with an art material, such as clay. This question usually results in silence or "I don't know . . ." Uneasy with this uncertainty, adults will often insist on directing the way. "Why don't you make a pinch pot?" It's all too easy for adults to overdo and undo a child's creative choices.

OPEN-ENDED ART

So how do we know if a program is conducive to creativity? One simple way to determine the creative potential of an art experience is to inquire if it is open-ended. Is the experience based primarily on the choices of the participant or the ideas of a group leader? Open-ended art experiences—with no step-by-step directions or examples of a specific end product—will offer the possibility for choice-based creative responses.

Also, many experiences intended to "teach" art can actually have few or no creative components at all, especially those requiring imitating the art products of adult artists. Although these experiences can perhaps train adult artists in technique, it is not advisable for young children to be required to copy adult art. This is not the way to develop art appreciation, art skills, or creativity. Indeed, expecting a group of young children to copy adult art (especially those of master artists) can be quite damaging to creative confidence rather than enhancing it. Rather than imitating an adult artist's artwork, children can be inspired by the *creative practice* of the artist. As educator Charles Schwall explains, "This happens when children are introduced to an artist's thought processes, motivations, and material techniques, and then given the freedom to discover the paths of their own work. This approach to teaching respects the work of the children and the artist equally" (Schwall 2015, 167–168).

The renowned art educator Robert Henri further explained, "It is useless to study technique in advance of having a motive. Instead of establishing a vast stock of technical tricks, it would be far wiser to develop creative power" (Henri 2007, 218).

Creative inspiration, for instance, can be found in the artwork of artist Georgia O'Keeffe. Children looking through the perspective of her paintings can wonder closely at flowers, or gaze up at New York skyscrapers or into a starlit sky through the branches of a ponderosa pine tree. By looking at art, like reading a book, we are seeing through the eyes of another. When we understand motivation, we shift perspective and thereby gain insight and empathy. What does the artist want us to see? What do we now see in another way? How can this be shown to others?

Learning to facilitate creative thought, rather than teach art, is the objective. In creative art groups, school-age children are offered the invitation to choose their own way. This inspiration is an enticement to learn through discovery.

Children learn best when they teach themselves, led by their own curiosity and inspired to pursue their own interests. This is true of all stages of life, but it is never more apparent than in the early years of childhood. Often the young children who are most curious about dinosaurs can pronounce their complex names and draw various dinosaurs from memory. Following curiosity to make discoveries is a highly effective way to learn and to enjoy the process all along the way.

THE ART OF PICTURE BOOKS

This question may be asked from the beginning: what does art have to do with libraries, anyway? Take a walk through the children's department; the answer is all around. If you stand in the center of the library stacks of picture books, select one—any one—book. Open it. What is seen first? The illustrations. Spanning the pages, the art may be humorous, light, and playful, or dark, serious, and subdued. Whether it is minimalist or intricately detailed, bold with color or subtly rendered with delicate tints, this *is* art. It is the art of children's literature. There are thousands of books surrounding you. Each one is *primarily* art. The words are secondary. It almost seems too obvious to say, but this is why it is called a *picture* book. Yes, the old saying is true: a picture *is* worth a thousand words.

Author and illustrator Barbara Cooney was twice the recipient of the Caldecott Award. Regarding how words and pictures come together, she once compared the picture book to a string of pearls and stated that "the pearls represent the illustrations, and the string represents the printed text" (Kiefer 1995, 6).

Clearly, Barbara Cooney valued the "pearls" of illustrations more than the "string" of words that bound them. Why, then, are picture books cataloged under the name of the author rather than the illustrator? Do libraries always place more value on words? It seems so, but there is an exception. The Eric Carle Museum of Picture Book Art in Massachusetts has a library where each picture book is alphabetized under the name of the *illustrator*, not the author. This may seem to be a radical idea, but why is the work of the illustrator not honored above that of the author of a *picture* book?

The fact that early childhood literature consists mainly of the art of illustration can be a startling idea, even for children's librarians. It can be a revelation for those who define books as words. The illustrations are the primary language of a picture book.

Wordless picture books. How can we possibly use them in storytime? Well, these books are intended to open the imagination. You can tell the story, but better yet, the *children* can tell the story in their own way. It is well known that children can "read" pictures long before they can read words. This allows storytime to evolve from a mostly passive experience into a mostly active one. It also allows for creative interpretation on the part of the children, which leads the way to a creative art experience during storytime.

FROM MAKING CRAFTS TO CREATING ART

What came before the concept of having an art studio in the library? As in most libraries across the country, there were occasional arts and crafts programs and always a craft after every storytime. There was a long-held tradition of just allowing 10 minutes for this craft activity. These "cute" crafts (designed and precut by adults) usually were related to the theme, such as assembling penguin crafts after winter storytime.

It became apparent to some of the library staff that these craft projects were often too difficult for young children to construct "properly" without the assistance of adult caregivers.

The penguins shown in Figure 2.1 are an example of the contrast between a craft assembled by an adult and one that looks more like those typically made by young children. The second one somewhat resembles a "Picasso" penguin! Of course, when children do something like this, they are not making mistakes by failing to follow the example of an adult. Young children do not see "penguin parts" in the unassembled pieces. So the rules are irrelevant and it is a whole lot of fun to glue randomly!

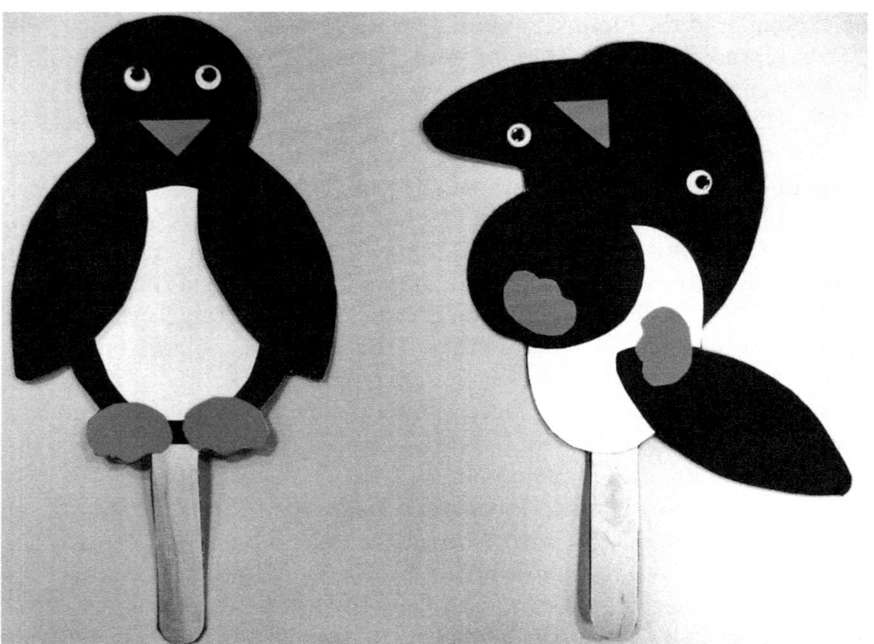

Figure 2.1 Craft Penguins: Author's samples.

Even so, all too often, parents or caregivers would apologize for what the child was doing and try to take over. A few adults scornfully dictated the "right" way, and some went so far as to undo the child's pasting to "fix" it, resulting in the child's tears of frustration. Scenes like this strengthened the resolve of the staff to change what we were doing. Now when we think back, all those Picasso Penguins were trying to tell us something. They *were* expressive art. We just needed to receive the message.

Simply stated, individual choices and ideas were being discouraged when assembling crafts. If the directions were not followed, it came out all wrong. Sameness was honored and rewarded. This craft is the *opposite* of a creative art experience, where unique responses and originality are encouraged. This is why art groups were designed that were age appropriate and enabled child-led art exploration.

We learned how to go beyond providing assembly crafts to offering creative art groups. Many of the materials were the same, starting basically with paper, glue, scissors, and markers. The difference was in *us*, not in the materials we presented. Before, with assembly crafts, the staff spent a considerable amount of time in precutting and preparing materials. An adult example of a finished product was always shown to the group with exact instructions on how to use the pieces to assemble them correctly. Alternatively, as facilitators of creativity groups, we did not prepare precut projects requiring specific directions to complete. When the emphasis was placed on the art process, there were no examples of finished products at all. Instead, freely exploring art materials resulted in unique self-guided experiences.

Another obvious way to differentiate assembly craft groups from creative art groups is to observe: do the products all look exactly the same—or very similar? Under this criterion, many experiences disguised as "art" are actually assembly craft experiences. With a discerning eye searching online sites, it is surprising how many rigidly structured multistep craft lessons are listed as "creative." This can also apply to highly structured art lessons. If the goal is to copy art or to learn perspective by reproducing a drawing of train tracks merging at the horizon, there is little chance for creative choices. Skills such as perspective can be learned through a myriad of self-directed choices of subject matter. Whether drawing a landscape, a truck, or a pair of shoes, each can teach elements of perspective. When we work from our own ideas and interests, choice deepens intrinsic motivation. The process will be far more engaging, and the results will be much more rewarding.

Another way to discern if an art experience allows for choice is to examine how many specific directions are required to be followed exactly. An art experience with a high degree of creative choice would provide minimal directions. For example, it may be enough to just say "explore and create!"

A creativity facilitator thus opens options rather than restricts them by carefully choosing what to say, knowing that the intent is to support decision making, autonomy, resourcefulness, and creative confidence. The aim is to open up imaginative possibilities. Trust each group member to take the lead. This often means that we as facilitators learn how to get out of the way of the creative process. We stand by to respond when necessary. If this is done well, you will be surprised how little you have to do and say and how intensely groups will invest in even the simplest of art explorations. Very few will ask you for help. You will witness people of all ages spending long periods of time exploring oil pastels, painting with one color, modeling a small amount of clay, or placing paper fragments on a collage.

When presenting an art material to a group for the first time, such as oil pastels, go just a little further with the invitation to explore: "These are oil pastels. Try them on light and on dark paper. They can be layered and blended." No directions at all are necessary if the material is familiar to the group. "What can you create with these materials?" can be an inspiring prompt. This way, a table set with inviting collage materials will not limit the participant to just pasting what is before them; they will explore beyond. Some group members may decide to bend and shape the paper to form three-dimensional sculptures or assemblages. To invite this level of creativity, have a variety of other tools readily accessible. Scissors, tape, staplers, string, and a hole punch will open up a dazzling array of potential responses. Essentially, all these materials are readily available in a craft area. The difference is how they are presented. Ask yourself, do I really need to control the outcome? Or do I trust the creative process?

THE ART OF SIMPLICITY

If you wish to facilitate creativity, strive for simplicity. Doing less offers more. Providing art materials with invitingly open expectations will enable group members to make choices that lead in vastly different directions. Oil pastels may be used to depict a fruit bowl or an interstellar space battle. Instructions that point only one way will obstruct these diverse creative responses. Try instead to offer guidelines that open up alternatives. Encourage investigation of hidden possibilities. Trust that this will lead beyond expectations.

Invariably some people will ask, "What should I do?" If the response is "Do what you *want* to do," most will eagerly take this invitation to work from their own ideas. Others, however, may find this open invitation baffling and become increasingly perplexed. They have had little experience with open choice. They asked for directions because they feel lost. Rather than circle back to the problem, help them find their way out. The irony is that they are actually asking for guidance to find their *own* way. So how can we be helpful without taking the lead and telling them what to do? How do we not close down options but keep the choices as open-ended as possible?

There is a response that we will return to again and again. By simply saying, "Explore. Try experimenting with the art materials," the message between the lines is that play has been officially endorsed. It is okay not to make anything at all. Moreover, permission has been granted to make all sorts of mistakes and messes. Once the pressure is off to "make something good," then the fun can truly begin. Muddling and messing around will have a chance to lead to some unanticipated areas and some startling surprises. "Hey, these oil pastels are kind of like crayons, only better! I can blend them! Wow, I never knew this before!" An unpredictable outcome adds to the excitement. So what if mistakes are made or it never goes anywhere important? It is a self-guided art experience, one that goes in the direction of creativity. This is teaching creative thought, not teaching art.

Does this answer the question, "What should I do?" Yes and no. It is answered in a nonrestrictive way. We have set up an environment that is conducive to taking chances and invites play. Then we get out of the way so that everyone can play freely. We step aside but do not disappear from view. Facilitators of creativity provide encouragement for others to move forward on their own, while we follow at a distance to be there when needed.

LESS IS TRULY MORE: SIMPLICITY AND FLEXIBILITY

Designing an art-based creativity program may seem intimidating. But less is more. Becoming less complicated, however, is not easy. Facilitating creativity requires a balance of contradictions.

Ironically, planning is the key to spontaneity and flexibility. Learning when to be silent and listen intently is necessary to encourage expression in others. When we are not overly directive, others will have the chance to be led by their own curiosity and interests. When we are not being overly helpful, others have a chance to discover their own solutions to problems and direct their own explorations. Doing less becomes doing much more.

> True words seem paradoxical.
> —Lao Tzu, *Tao Te Ching*, Chapter 78

Even the choice of music in an art room is best guided by minimalism. Music that is too boisterous, dramatic, or complex may distract concentration and drown out conversation. It is also advisable to avoid "children's music" or "elevator music" that is trite and unsophisticated. Simple acoustic renditions of traditional folk and world music have been well received in the art room. Soft chamber music, cool jazz, piano solos, even classical renditions of lullabies will subtly enhance the environment and lift or soothe spirits. Usually music should fall into the background; an exception would be when the art making is intended to be directly influenced by the sounds being heard, such as during a "painting to music" session. Yet even when it is barely detectable in the background, music is an influential aspect of the ambiance and is best chosen with care and respect for all those who will be listening.

Although less is more, these art experiences are never to be mistaken for "passive programming." Open art is the opposite. A facilitator of creativity is active, alert, and highly engaged even at a distance—ever attentive, observant, and attuned to what is happening in the group. Scanning moment by moment, the facilitator evaluates when to step forward to assist and when to step away. A facilitator evaluates what to say and, even more importantly, what *not* to say. A facilitator models creativity through flexibility, openness to diverse ideas, and the courage to take chances and to learn from mistakes.

When thought becomes flexible, mistakes can be viewed as valuable learning experiences, leading to the development of resilience and confidence. When accidents occur, such as a spill on the floor, it is best to normalize these mishaps. Mistakes are

> Failure is an opportunity.
> —Lao Tzu, *Tao Te Ching*, Chapter 79

to be expected and most are quite simple to fix. When children are invited to take part in the cleanup, they learn how easily problems can be resolved, especially when working together. This will be especially important for children inhibited by fears of mistakes and messes. When a child learns to be flexible, an accidental splotch of paint on the paper is not a disaster. Instead, it can be the inspiration for a new idea. What an empowering notion! Seeming mistakes can open the way to further exploration and invite more adventurous risk-taking and experimentation. As cartoonist Scott Adams observed, "Creativity is allowing yourself to make mistakes. Art is knowing which ones to keep" (Adams 1996, 324).

Most of all, a facilitator will radiate the spirit of wonder and joy that invites others to cross the threshold into creative experiences. But before any of us can take a new direction, we must leave familiar territory behind. This may not happen all at once. We have been taught to retrace the well-worn paths that lead to predictable places. In order to begin anew, we first "unlearn" that this is the only way to go. This can be difficult. Unlearning demands that we let go of long-held cherished beliefs, admit that missteps were made, and resolve to take another way. Sometimes this seems like going backward, losing ground, and even losing our way. Yet we must lose the safety of familiar ground to go beyond what we have done before. This new experience will take us to the creative edge. It is always just outside our comfort zone. It takes courage to go there.

EXTENDING MAKING INTO CREATING

Resistance to creativity is to be expected, from within ourselves and from those around us. Places such as libraries have been eager to invest in change through technology. The term "making" has often been used interchangeably with "creating." This making is usually the product of technology, tools, or toys. What is "created" is mostly made by computers and machines or built with constructing toys. Investments have been made in these spaces for making, but these investments can also be extended to places for creating. It is time to balance technology with creativity. It is time to balance information with inspiration. It is time to invest in hands-on experiences for all ages and levels of ability, beginning with the basic creative needs of very young children.

If we invest in creativity, someday it will yield far more than we can calculate. But it is not necessary to speculate on future earnings. All we need is to focus on here and now for the value to become apparent. Spend one afternoon with children involved in a creative art experience. You do not need to tell them what to do. In fact, the more you tell them what to do, the less creative it will be for them. This is not about *your* ideas. It is about *their* ideas. If you learn to listen much more than you speak, children will learn much more than you could ever teach.

True mastery can be gained by letting things go their own way. It can't be gained by interfering.

—Lao Tzu, *Tao Te Ching,* Chapter 48

INVITING THE UNEXPECTED

Those who facilitate creativity in an open art studio program exemplify the components of creativity by inviting the unexpected. If the venue is a library, then this program will be unlike any other. Rather than be instructed by a leader and regimented by plans that are strictly followed within short time constraints, flexibility will be the key. Rather than divided by ages, all generations will be invited into Open Art Studio. Rather than limited to an hour, the studio will be open for extended lengths of time, with people coming and going throughout the session. Some participants may stay for 20 minutes, while others remain for hours.

Since all ages are welcome, planning for diverse skill levels will be a necessity. How can any art experience be meaningful for everyone—from toddler to teen to adult—all at the same time? The answer is not complexity but simplicity. It is best to avoid complex art experiences. Simply providing folded paper and markers is an excellent place to begin. Include envelopes, and the "lost art" of designing and sending cards is revived, much to the delight of everyone!

An open-ended art experience, however, can imaginatively go far beyond this. During collage and card-making sessions, children have asked for additional materials so they can develop their own ideas. When staff provided scissors, glue, string, and tape, the children surprised us with pop-ups, foldouts, small books, even a working bird marionette! (Fletcher 2016, 11–12).

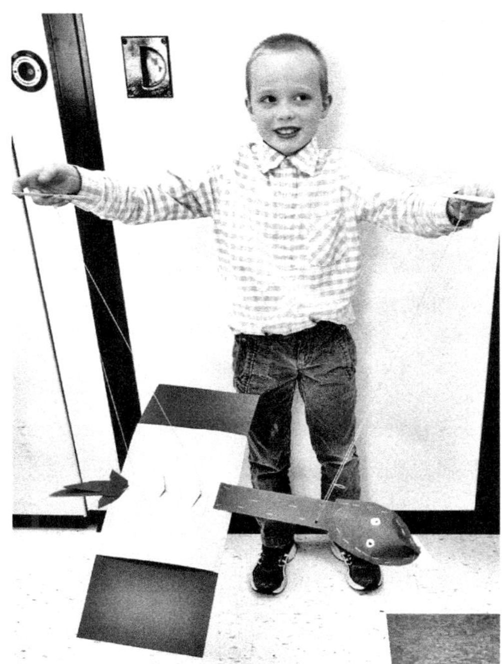

Figure 2.2   Artwork by William Olmstead.

PROCESS ART

Process art is the self-guided exploration of art materials based on curiosity and the joy of learning through discovery. The benefit of such art experiences for toddlers through preschool has been widely accepted. There are excellent resources available on this subject, and many notable books by author MaryAnn Kohl have emphasized the process rather than the product. She advocates giving children art materials that are interesting and watching what they will do. In her words, "Process art is a wonder to behold. Watch the children discover their capabilities and the joy of creativity" (Kohl 1994, 11). Kohl is also an advocate for older siblings and parents exploring process art (5).

Art experiences that value the process can be freeing and expansive for all ages. These encounters are usually based solely on exploration and experimentation with art materials. Most of all, process art values the experience—the outcome is not the main objective.

Process art is analogous to a canoe trip. A trip down a river these days is not about getting from one place to another. There certainly are far more efficient means of travel. It is all about the adventure. It is about going into the flow and away from familiar routine. Entering the unknown, however, can turn out to be not so much calming, as it is challenging. Our senses will not be soothed but instead intensified and sharpened. We are never more involved in the here and now than when we lose track of time. Aware of the beauty all around us, suddenly we take a turn. Now we move more swiftly as we navigate around obstacles with the risk of being overturned. The angle and force of each stroke is a guiding choice. We must be vigilant along the way for peril and unexpected wonders. So it is not about what we will see when we arrive. It is about being connected to the flow of experience and ever moving onward.

This is how it feels to be involved in a process. Very young children lead the way joyfully in process experiences, inexhaustible and blissfully unaware that they are meandering. Adults are inclined to want to stay on course and find the fastest way to destinations. We take the quickest way to work, the most efficient route to do errands, and the straightest highway to get to our vacation spot. We get stuck in the fast lane and become bored, annoyed, and then infuriated on our drives. We try to block out the experience with music, the news, and movies for the kids in the back seat. How many of us have driven on the highway only to have very little memory of the experience? Taking part in the process is being aware of the ride.

By the time we become adults, many of us have lost the joy of the journey. It is all about efficiency. It is about not wasting time, not risking getting lost. We set our GPS to get somewhere as soon as possible. The fastest methods of doing everything are preferred. Even on vacation we speed in the fast lane and stop only for gas and fast food. We are in such a hurry to get somewhere that we get frustrated by anything that slows us down. We do not have time for anything along the way. Lost are all the enriching experiences along the winding backroads through the shade forests and across the sun-drenched farmlands.

> A good traveller has no fixed plans
> and is not intent upon arriving.
> A good artist lets his intuition
> Lead him wherever it wants.
> A good scientist has freed himself of concepts
> and keeps his mind open to what is.
>
> —Lao Tzu, *Tao Te Ching*, Chapter 27

PROCESS AND THE LOVE OF LEARNING

Somewhere along the way, we were all taught to undervalue process and overvalue product. What becomes of the love of learning in our educational system? How often does that system instill dread instead? For many it does. School becomes just a means to an end, something to "get through" to get the degree and get the job. The job becomes something to "get through" to get the money. It seems we are always just trying to "get through" something to get to something else. When we think of it this way, we are always trying to get through a process to get to a product.

We have all been taught to undervalue process and overvalue product. Furthermore, with art it is all about products measured through the standards of "experts" who define quality in art. But art keeps transcending its own definition. This is as true of a poem as it is of a painting. As Thoreau once said, "The wisest definition of poetry the poet will instantly prove false by setting aside its requisitions" (Thoreau 1980, 91). So how do we define what is original and innovative according to preset standards? Do grades in art only appraise how skillfully one has followed the directions? Is there really an objective criterion to make artistic value judgments regarding originality? Are grades just an aesthetic opinion? And, when it comes to young children, should art be graded at all?

There is much to be gained by freely taking part in a process—such as dance, for instance—and the experience becomes its own reward. Expression through movement is inspiriting and exhilarating. For most of us, the pleasure would be diminished if our performances were always graded, negatively compared to others, or measured according to professional standards. Believing we lack ability becomes a self-fulfilling prophecy. We become uncertain, self-conscious, awkward, and constricted. We feel embarrassed to express ourselves in this way and reluctant even to make an attempt. Some of us would avoid ever dancing again. The joy is lost.

Process Is Dancing Freely—Dancing for Joy

One advantage of doing art programs in a library is that it is not school. It is not limited by the requirements of an educational system. The art will not be graded or critiqued. The participants are not in competition with one another. This alone places emphasis on the learning experience, rather than on the result of that experience. With painting, for instance, it is the active process of "painting" as a verb that is emphasized, rather than the noun "painting" as the product outcome of that experience.

Most adults have never made art in a nonjudgmental setting. This freedom can be a powerful motivator for those who have never experienced it before. Those who say they stopped making art long ago, usually say that it is because they were told that they were not very "good" at it. They used to love art, but sometime in elementary school they stopped. Their art abilities halted at that level for the rest of their lives.

It is no wonder why adult coloring and doodling have become so popular. Those who were fond of these activities in childhood and adolescence are now freed to revisit and practice these skills. These experiences are highly structured, and this explains why some people find them so appealing and enjoyable. A need is satisfied by filling in the blanks, which continuously gives a sense of accomplishment. Some find serenity during this process, which has been likened to a meditative state. This is restorative and gratifying. But it is not necessary to stop here. The door can be opened to more challenging realms where the risks are higher and so are the rewards.

OPENING UP POSSIBILITIES

Art-based creativity programming can be offered through various approaches:

Process art is the self-guided exploration of art materials.

Open-ended art is an idea, theme, or surface, such as a mask that inspires creative interpretations.

Collaborative art is a group project with an overall theme and a choice-based component. For instance, in creating a mural of a town, everyone contributes a house of their own design. Each individual contribution is unique.

Of course, each of these methods is not entirely distinct from one another. The lines are often blurred among these approaches during a single art session. For example, participants will take part in a creative project or collaborative art and then be encouraged to use the same art materials to work entirely from their own ideas. Overall, creativity programming will place value on process, choice, and opening up possibilities.

To understand creativity, we must first understand what it is and what it is not. To facilitate creativity, we must know what has been done and what has been left undone in terms of nurturing creativity in children. The following chapters will often refer to the writings of neuroscientists, psychologists, educators, leaders in innovation, and experts in child development, the arts, and creativity. This will be only a sampling of the theorists, researchers, and practitioners who have made major contributions to our understanding of what it means to be creative. Often quoted to keep in their own words, these authors speak with an eloquence that would be difficult to state in any other way. At times their prose ascends to the poetic to become a work of art in itself.

3

Theory, Research, and Practice

THE LANGUAGE OF ART

The need to create art—to make our mark—has been with us since the dawn of consciousness. Drawings documented our thoughts long before written language evolved from them. This is true of ancient beings and it is true of children today. Children create images long before they write words. We are all drawn to mark-making from the beginning.

Human beings with the skills to symbolize ideas painted on the walls of caves well over 30,000 years ago. These images found in Europe, Indonesia, and elsewhere around the globe are actually not *pre*historic, because art marks our history. Ancient art reaches through time as a living language that "speaks" to us now. We understand through the eloquence of the art: the passing form of an extinct creature, the forward motion, the implied movement of the legs, the elegant contoured line that vividly holds the surging essence of a once living being. There is no need to decipher a dead language, no obscure text to translate. Long before the written word, art expressed ideas that have pierced through the ages to penetrate us now. We comprehend simply by seeing the images of the painted and engraved walls of Lascaux, Chauvet, and Pech Merle in Southern France. We can imagine walking now through caves such as these. There are lions in profile, bison, and rhinos. Here is a mammoth. There are deer and ancient dappled horses . . . and there is the form of a human hand. Perhaps the signature of the artist.

WE ARE KNOWN BY WHAT WE CREATE

Many of today's children will live well into the 22nd century. They will be elders in a world we can only imagine. If change continues to accelerate at this bewildering rate, it will be a world of inconceivable complexity. While some of our current problems may no longer exist, the solutions may have led to unforeseen consequences and possibly far more difficult problems to solve.

No one can deny that what is done now—or not done—will impact the future. The consensus among scientists, psychologists, and educators is that it is vital to raise children with creative minds. Many say that our very survival on this planet may depend upon it. Psychologist and researcher Mihaly Csikszentmihalyi cautions, "There is no question that the human species could not survive, either now or in the years to come, if creativity were to run dry. Scientists will have to come up with new solutions to over-population, the depletion of nonrenewable resources, and the pollution of the environment—or the future will indeed be brutish and short. . . . Whether we like it or not, our species has become dependent on creativity" (Csikszentmihalyi 1996, 317–318).

Fortunately, resources exist to develop creative skills in ourselves and our children. Research has found that this capacity for creativity is within us all. Anyone reading these words has creative potential, and these abilities can go far beyond what has been previously realized. "Indeed, creativity contributes to development," according child development psychologist Mark Runco. He adds, "It is in some ways inextricable from development, just as it is inextricable from human nature. It may sound like a cliché, but it is nonetheless true that to be creative is to be human and to be open to development" (Runco 1996, 89).

According to author Daniel H. Pink, an expert and lecturer on business and politics, "The last few decades have belonged to a certain kind of person with a certain kind of mind—computer programmers who could crank code, lawyers who could craft contracts, MBAs who could crunch numbers. But the keys to the kingdom are changing hands. The future belongs to a very different kind of person with a very different kind of mind—creators and empathizers, pattern recognizers, and meaning makers. These people—artists, inventors, designers, storytellers, caregivers, consolers, big picture thinkers—will now reap society's richest rewards and share its greatest joys" (Pink 2005, 1).

PUTTING THE "A" INTO STEM

Many educators have recognized the need to infuse the arts and creativity into the sciences. STEM stands for science, technology, engineering, and math. STEAM adds the A for arts: visual arts, music, drama, and dance. Integration of arts-related skills with the sciences has been found to be a way to increase student motivation and to deepen learning. Yet with budget constraints and emphasis to teach to the test, the arts are on the decline in schools. In their book *From STEM to STEAM,* author David A. Sousa and arts educator Tom Pilecki advocate for the arts in education and strongly support the integration of the arts into other areas of the curriculum. "Now, pressure to improve reading and mathematics achievement is prompting elementary schools to trade instruction in the arts for more classroom time in preparation for high-stakes testing. . . . This trade-off does not make sense in light of the emerging research on how the arts assist in developing the young brain." The authors emphatically state, "Schools have an obligation to expose children to the arts at the earliest possible time and to consider the arts as a fundamental—not an optional—curriculum area" (Sousa and Pilecki 2013, 14–15).

There is, as Sousa and Pilecki confirm, "convincing evidence from research studies in cognitive and social neuroscience that demonstrate how activities associated with the arts enhance creativity, problem solving, memory systems, motor coordination, and analytical skills—all critical elements to achieving the STEM objectives" (3).

There are many sources for ideas that present hands-on projects for kids that cross the boundaries between the arts and sciences. *STEAM Kids* is authored by a diverse group of engineers, architects, and art teachers, among others, who contributed over 50 STEAM activity ideas. These experiences help children learn such things as the science of bubbles and playful experimentation: the history of mandalas and circular patterns using natural objects, and the life cycle of plants through recording observations of their growth, making sun prints, or drawing shadow changes over a period of time (Carey et al. 2016).

For instance, when children depict dinosaurs, construct fortresses, sketch from nature, or imaginatively design an intergalactic spacecraft, these activities extend STEM into STEAM. Furthermore, Sousa and Pilecki contend, "When learners see no boundaries limiting fields of study, creativity and genius often flourish" (92). The arts can be a motivating force bringing meaning and even joy into exploring science, technology, engineering, and math. The freedom to explore and creatively connect ideas across fields is the key to solving problems through innovation. Practicing arts-related skills of close observation, inquiry, and discovery will give insight into the creative process of inventors in technology, scientific research, and beyond.

With all the potential benefits of integrating the arts, still there is reluctance to do so. Many adults, even educators, still believe that creativity is a fixed trait that cannot be changed. One is creative or one is not creative.

Teachers have passed this mistaken belief on to their students. "But in recent years," Sousa and Pilecki counter, "scientists have found that creativity is part of human nature—hardwired into all of our brains . . . we all possess creativity to some degree, and the great news is that we can get better at it" (53).

WIRED TO CREATE

According to neurological research, our brains are indeed wired to create. Furthermore, it is now considered a myth that creativity takes place only in the right region of the brain. "The creative process draws on the *whole* brain," explained psychologist Scott Barry Kaufman and Carolyn Gregoire in their book *Wired to Create.* People who are creative demonstrate flexibility in their ability to activate and deactivate brain networks, while being able to balance modes of thought that seem to be in opposition. With all these interacting cognitive systems, creativity is certainly complex. "Even on a *neurological* level, creativity is messy" (Kaufman and Gregoire 2015, xxvi–xxix). The authors propose, "Being creative requires the cultivation of a balance of skills—including the ability to learn and memorize—as well as the ability to *free oneself* from that knowledge and from habitual ways of thinking in order to imagine possibilities that have never been dreamed of before" (xxxii).

Kaufman and Gregoire conclude that "creativity works in mysterious and often paradoxical ways. . . . It is both deliberate and uncontrollable, mindful and mindless, work and play. It is both the realm of a select group of geniuses through history, and the domain of every human being." We are all encouraged to accept our own creativity before we can be able to extend it to others. The authors maintain, "When we embrace our own messiness—engaging with the world with our own unique imagination and artistry—we give others permission to do the same. We help create a world that is more welcoming of the creative spirit and, it is hoped, make it possible to find a greater connection with ourselves and others in the process" (185).

CREATIVITY AND INNOVATION

Tom Kelley, general manager of IDEO, an international product design company, believes that anyone can be creative. Overcoming fear of failure is an important objective at IDEO. He refers to "joyful failures" as a part of taking chances and risks. Kelley reasons, "Failure is the flip side of risk taking, and if you don't risk, odds are you won't succeed" (Kelley and Littman 2001, 232–235).

He has made it a goal to create an environment in the workplace that is conducive to innovation by encouraging the free expression of ideas, brainstorming, taking chances, rule breaking, and a spirit of play. "A playful, iterative approach to problems is one of the foundations of our culture," Kelley remarks, "a lot of us understood this intuitively as children and lost it gradually as we matured" (105). The key is to learn how to tap into this childlike curiosity and enthusiasm as adults.

Drawing out ideas in brainstorming is more than just talking openly about ideas. Kelley observed that—

> Once you start drawing or making things, you open up new possibilities of discovery. It's the same method that's helped scientists unlock some of the greatest secrets of nature . . . helped guide them toward the momentous discovery of the structure of DNA . . . Doodling, drawing, modeling. Sketch ideas and make things, and you're likely to encourage accidental discoveries. At the most fundamental level, what we're talking about is play, about exploring borders. (Kelley and Littman 2001, 108–109)

WHY WE RESIST CREATIVE CHANGE

There is an undeniable need for creative minds that is not limited to the arts, but extends into the fields of science, technology, business, education, and beyond. Creativity consultant Jennifer Mueller maintains, "We have serious problems to solve: global warming, terrorism, pollution, nuclear threats, and more. . . . How do we find solutions? *Creativity*" (Mueller 2017, ix).

Despite the fact that businesses invest millions on creativity consultants and workshops, there is often resistance to new ideas. Mueller's book *Creative Change: Why We Resist It . . . How We Can Embrace It* explores the reasoning behind the barriers that impede creative change despite the need for it. She found that America is facing a "creativity crisis" based on a lack of creative leadership. Widespread misunderstanding about what it means to be creative is perpetuated in our school systems. She specified that "if elementary school teachers equate creativity with the arts—which they believe are important, but not essential for education—what message do you think teachers send to the next generation of leaders?" (175).

Yet even if the definition of creativity is broadened, there remains resistance to new ideas and innovation. This is because creative ideas are not proven. Creativity involves risk. In Mueller's words, "Decades of research shows that people dislike and want to avoid uncertainty . . . creative ideas are uncertain . . . I believe this is the essence of why it is so difficult to make creative change, and why creative change is the hidden barrier in the innovation chain" (14). Although it is possible to get past this barrier, it will never entirely go away.

So, creativity means leaving certainty behind. No wonder it takes courage.

Society may always shun its own creative agents of change, according to psychologist and researcher Ruth Richards. It is not as easy as it may seem to counter this bias, even within ourselves. In order to facilitate creativity, we must understand the challenges of sustaining an environment conducive to divergent thoughts and creative choices. Richards asserted, "Freedom, self-discovery, discovery of the world and one's ability to act in it. Sounds fine. But there is also a well-known price for the adult who works with such creative children. These kids will not always behave in ways an adult might predict or prefer" (Richards 1996, 68).

Creative behaviors may be labeled noncompliant. Flights of fantasy and imagination may be considered being off-task and daydreaming. Expressing and acting on original ideas may be perceived as not following the directions and deviating from the norm. Frequently asking questions can be interpreted as disrespectful and even as challenging authority.

Adults who truly value childhood creativity need to be supportive by "attending to and facilitating the developing child's marvelous modes of thought," according to Richards. This will benefit not only the child but also the adult. She explains, "There is also a great deal we can reclaim for ourselves in this pursuit. For it is truly by retaining the mind of the child—with all its openness, wonder, sensitivity, and surprise—along with the guiding skills of the adult, that we can create the greatest 'evolution of creativity,' and the greatest hope for the world of the future" (83).

WHO IS CREATIVE?

> **Cre•a•tive** \krē-'ā-tiv, 'krē-,\ *adj* (1678) **1** : marked by the ability or power to create : given to creating < the ~ impulse > **2** : having the quality of something created rather than imitated : IMAGINATIVE < the ~ arts >

This definition of "creative" is in the first two entries of *Merriman-Webster's Collegiate Dictionary*. But from this, do we understand what it means to be creative? Defining will not be so easy. Views of creativity are so diverse that some seem contradictory. Some perspectives focus primarily on the accomplishments of extraordinary adults capable of making a significant impact on the world—as most vividly seen in the art world. Other perspectives offer a wider and more inclusive view that creativity spans far beyond the arts and infuses everyday experience. Then creativity is seen less in terms of product and more as process. In definitions that emphasize the creative process, not only adults are considered truly creative but also children. Children may, perhaps, be the most creative of us all.

If, indeed, we all have creative potential and capacities, then these abilities can be nurtured and developed. We can *choose* to be creative and learn how to be more creative throughout our lives. Creating is learning. Lifelong learning. When we are creating, we are in the process of becoming more complete and fulfilled human beings. We are expanding at the creative edge of our capacities. We are becoming more than we were before.

Pediatrician and psychoanalyst D. W. Winnicott once defined creativity simply as "the doing that arises out of being." He professed, "Whatever definition we arrive at, it must include the idea that life is worth living or not, according to whether creativity is or is not a part of an individual person's living experience" (Winnicott 1986, 39).

Psychologist Mihaly Csikszentmihalyi spent decades researching creativity and states of "optimal experience" that enrich the quality of our lives and give meaning to our existence. He revealed, "Contrary to what we usually believe . . . the best moments in our lives, are not the passive, receptive, relaxing times. . . . The best moments usually occur when a person's body or mind is stretched to its limits in a voluntary effort to accomplish something difficult and worthwhile. Optimal experience is thus something that we *make* happen. For a child, it could be placing with trembling fingers the last block on a tower she has built, higher than any she has built so far. . . . For each person there are thousands of opportunities, challenges to expand ourselves" (Csikszentmihalyi 1990, 3).

UNDERSTANDING THE SIGNIFICANCE OF CREATIVITY

Psychologist Rollo May was an educator at Harvard, Princeton, and Yale. In his influential book, *The Courage to Create,* he maintained that the creative process represents "the highest degree of emotional health." May added that, "one must not rule out the extent to which it is present in captains of modern technology as well as in a mother's normal relationship with her child" (May 1975, 33).

How then do we quantify the value of these experiences that are so integral to being human, so enduring, so vast, and seemingly immeasurable? Art has illustrated human history. How do we begin to study creativity if it is so vast? Author Robert Paul Weiner, in his book *Creativity and Beyond,* states that "to a considerable extent, world history *is* the history of creativity. But our common modern conception of creativity is itself a new creation" (Weiner, 2000, 1).

Very few scientific investigations into creativity were conducted before the second half of the 20th century. One reason may have been that science recognizes and values only what is measurable, but how can we measure creativity? Standards had long been established for studying academic abilities, but creativity was far more elusive. It may have seemed to be more of a *quality* than a quantity to be measured. When studies of creativity began, it was approached in myriad ways: as a set of abilities, attitudes, or personality traits that enabled ingenuity, imaginative problem-solving, inventiveness and other capacities. Through this varied research, creativity began to be understood not as a rare gift of genetic inheritance but as a set of *skills* that could be developed under the right circumstances. With this came the understanding that creativity requires practice. If the environment does not offer these opportunities, creative abilities that once existed can diminish. Conversely, in an environment conducive to practicing creativity, these skills can be enhanced.

Author Jonah Lehrer has explored the scientific research that has given us new insight into creative minds. He states, "The first thing this new perspective makes clear is that the standard definition of *creativity* is completely wrong. Ever since the ancient Greeks, people have assumed that the imagination is separate from other kinds of cognition. But the latest science suggests that this assumption is false (Lehrer 2012, xvii). "Creativity," he explained, "shouldn't be thought of as a process reserved for artists and inventors and other 'creative types.' The human mind, after all, has the creative impulse built into its operating system, hard-wired into its most essential programming code. At any given moment, the brain is automatically forming new associations, continually connecting an everyday x to an unexpected y" (xx).

So if creativity is an everyday—even an every-moment experience—why do so many of us believe we are not creative? Julia Cameron, best-selling author on creativity, cautions us that we are misinforming children when we deny our own creative capacity. "When we tell our children that we are not creative, our children learn that there is such a thing as 'not being creative,' which is deeply untrue. Once they have this (mis)information, it is a short walk to their repeating it about themselves. You are creative. Your child is creative. . . . Be thoughtful when you respond to their art" (Cameron and Lively 2013, 155–156).

Children need adults to model creativity. Many of these adults, however, were taught to believe that they were not artistic or creative in early elementary school. "When youngsters are daunted early and unfairly because of their inability to conform to a norm that is not their own, a long road to creative recovery is paved ahead of them," according Cameron. As a result, "many creatives who are routinely squelched in academic settings languish for years in the wake of these shaming experiences" (203). Creative recovery involves rediscovering the right to play, experiment, imagine, and express original ideas.

Before we can facilitate creativity in others, we must find it within ourselves. This requires courage because there is risk in expressing original ideas. Our ideas could be criticized, judged and graded as mediocre, substandard, or just downright bad. "Being wrongly shamed as creatives, we learn that we are wrong to create." Cameron urges, "We must, must be brave here . . . or we risk remaining blocked and discouraging our children as well" (208).

From this we can realize how detrimental it is to view creativity as being given only to an exclusive few. Just as intelligence does not only belong to geniuses, creativity does not only belong to those who have made extraordinary contributions to the arts, the sciences, and social change. Creativity is not limited to those who have been validated by recognition or prestige.

As the famous art educator Robert Henri explained, "Genius is not a possession of the limited few, but exists in some degree in everyone. Where there is natural growth, a full and free play of faculties, genius will manifest itself" (Henri 2007, 218). He went on to say, "We must get rid of this outside feeling of looking in on art. We must get on the inside and press out. . . . Any material will do. After all, the object is not to *make art*, but to be in that wonderful state which makes art inevitable. In every human being there is the artist" (224).

Many are still on the outside looking in at art. What is more, they refuse to accept that they can be creative in any way despite neuroscientific findings that place creativity at the core of what it means to be human. If we deny our own creative potential, we will give up possession of it. We will stop trying. Then indeed creativity will only be received by the select few, the "gifted" ones. Creativity belongs to us all. We must not give up our inherent right to be creative.

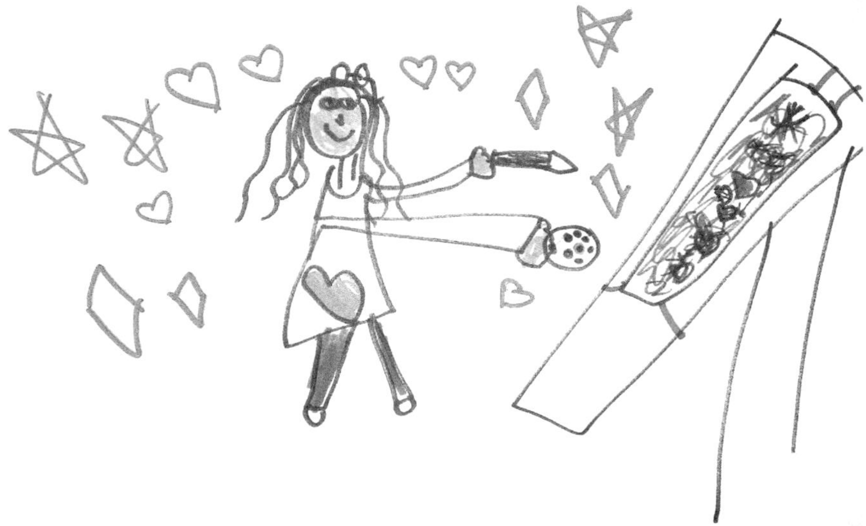

Figure 3.1 Artwork by Charlotte Sohn.

CREATIVE MINDS

Howard Gardner, in his influential book *Creating Minds*, observed that "we can discern the links to childhood that seem to run through the lives of highly creative individuals. As Einstein often pointed out, the problems he pondered were those that children spontaneously raise. . . . Only individuals still in touch with the experiences of childhood could have unraveled these phenomena" (134–135).

"The links to early childhood abound in the artistic realm," recounts Gardner. As exemplified by artists who seek to capture the "primitive and childlike" in their work. Gardner specified that "the modern masters centered their own work around the elements that are salient for the young child: Picasso around the rough scribbles and collagelike juxtaposition of the toddler." Gardner is careful to add, "My point is not to denigrate creative masters: it is to extol the amazing power of childhood, as well as its startling endurance, at least in certain individuals" (401–402).

How do we support this "amazing power of childhood" and enable it to endure? According to Gardner, we must be aware of those aspects of our current culture that threaten childhood. He strongly cautions that "children are exposed from early on to the knowledge, mysteries, wonders, and horrors of the world, perhaps childlike innocence must forever be sacrificed. No wonder that many pundits have spoken nostalgically, or with alarm, about the 'disappearance of childhood'" (404–405).

Neil Postman's book *The Disappearance of Childhood* contends that the unquestioning acceptance of technology as progress has become a directive of American culture. It is, therefore, an act of rebellion when parents attempt to control the media's access to their own children. Yet Postman advocates for this rebelliousness by adults, urging them to limit the time and to monitor the content of media exposure for children. "Both are very difficult to do and require a level of attention that most parents are not prepared to give to child-rearing." Postman acknowledged, "Nonetheless, there are parents who are committed to doing all of these things, who are in effect defying the directives of their culture. . . . It is not conceivable that our culture will forget that it needs children. But it is halfway toward forgetting that children need childhood. Those who insist on remembering shall perform a noble service" (Postman 1994, 153).

BEING CREATIVE EVERY DAY

We are all far more creative than we realize, according to psychologist and researcher Ruth Richards. It is our *everyday creativity* that is key to coping and thriving in the 21st century. But what is meant by everyday creativity? Richards explains, "It is the way you get through a day, find your way out of the woods, cope with a difficult boss, feed everyone when there's nothing to eat, help your child learn, and keep yourself sane" (Richards 2017, 13). We are creative every day. If we could only acknowledge how often we tap into our creative resources, it would heighten our awareness of ourselves and of our potential. If we deny our creativity, we are giving up our birthright.

Adults are called upon to nurture creativity. A child with "a creative edge," as described by Richards, "is encouraged to be independent, to ask questions. Maybe this youth plays freely, and is given many resources for doing so." But what about the young person who does not have such advantages? And what about the youth with difficult problems? By finding "creative outlets," Richards observes, a troubled young person can become "the resilient creator in miniature." By learning to cope through creativity, one can not only survive but also thrive (190–191). This creativity, according to Richards "can aid our 'conscious evolution,' empowering us in an ever more endangered world" (207). We can learn to use our abilities to face and overcome adversity, to make things better. Through creativity we are able "to 'see beyond' and envision new ways of being in this world" (171).

Humanistic psychologist A. H. Maslow, in his book *The Farther Reaches of Human Nature*, emphasized the importance of creativeness and placed it at the core of well-being. He revealed, "The concept of creativeness and the concept of the healthy, self-actualizing, fully human person seem to be coming closer and closer together, and may perhaps turn out to be the same thing." As a strong advocate of "Education-Through-Art," Maslow held that art could one day span education and be the paradigm for teaching reading, writing, math, and subjects across the curriculum (Maslow 1993, 55).

Over the last few decades, there have been some notable changes in teaching methods that reflect this need to foster creative thinking. Some of the professors at M.I.T. have moved away from the tradition of teaching facts—which quickly become obsolete—toward developing creative minds that are open to the unexpected, flexible, and innovative. This change in the process of education is most recognizable in the sciences, engineering, and technology. However, these new concepts can also be applied to educating leaders in business, industry, education, politics, social reform, and beyond.

Maslow states, "It is quite clear that we must teach them to be creative persons. . . . They must be people who are capable of coping with the inevitably rapid obsolescence of any new product, or of any old way of doing things. They must be people who will not fight change but who will anticipate it, and who can be challenged enough by it to enjoy it" (94). This attitude is open to the unknown and gives permission to let go, to be spontaneous, to imagine, and to enjoy. These childlike qualities have not been lost by adult creatives. What is more, they can choose to regress at will and have fun. This "voluntary regression" is considered a characteristic of mature and quite healthy individuals (89). Yes, at times they may even appear just a little "crazy" to others. "(Every really new idea looks crazy, at first)" as Maslow parenthetically reminded us. In fact, he considered creativity itself to be a kind of "intellectual play" that emerges from our deeper self (82).

Author Tina Seelig has a PhD in neuroscience and teaches on creativity at Stanford University. She observes,

> Creativity allows you to thrive in an ever changing world and unlocks a universe of possibilities. With enhanced creativity, instead of problems you see potential, instead of obstacles you see opportunities, and instead of challenges you see a chance to create breakthrough solutions. Look around and it becomes clear that the innovators among us are the ones succeeding in every arena, from science and technology to education and the arts. Nevertheless, creative problem solving is rarely taught in school, or even considered a skill you can learn. (Seelig 2012, 4)

She contends, "It is time to make creative thinking, just like the scientific method, a core part of our education from the time we are children, and to reinforce these lessons throughout our lives" (10).

CAN CREATIVITY BE TAUGHT?

If creativity is this important, then can we learn to be more creative? If the answer is yes, then how is this done? Educators have defined creativity in a way that makes it apparent that the components can be taught. Two experts in the field of education, Dona Matthews, PhD, and Joanne Foster, Ed.D., explain creativity in this way:

"Creativity is what happens when content mastery, divergent thinking, critical thinking, and communication skills all come together in balance, in the service of a goal . . . each of these components is teachable" (Matthews and Foster 2014, 35). An environment that develops these four "tangible" components will also nurture creativity.

The authors also agree with psychologist Robert Sternberg, who has proposed that to a large extent creativity is a *decision*. According to Sternberg, creativity is "the decision to be creative, the decision of how to be creative, and the implementation of these decisions" (Sternberg 2003, 91). It will be imperative for children to "decide for creativity" in order to face the challenges of the future.

Creativity involves intellectual ability, knowledge, styles of thinking, personality, motivation, and the environment, as well as the *decision* to use these resources. One may have internal creative resources but lack a supportive environment. Most environments have impediments to creativity. These may suppress or block creativity in many individuals but not in everyone. Others will decide to go beyond these obstacles. As Sternberg notes, "Creativity is as much a decision about and an attitude toward life as it is a matter of ability. Creativity is often obvious in young children, but it may be harder to find in older children and adults because their creative potential has been suppressed by a society that encourages intellectual conformity" (98).

Sir Ken Robinson is a renowned speaker on education and creativity. His influential TED talk "Do Schools Kill Creativity?" is now the most highly viewed talk in the history of TED with over 50 million views. Robinson summarized:

> The essence of that talk was that we're all born with immense natural talents, but by the time we've been through education far too many of us have lost touch with them. As I put it then, many highly talented, brilliant people think they're not because the thing they were good at in school wasn't valued or was actually stigmatized. The consequences are disastrous for individuals and for the health of our communities. (Robinson 2015, xviii)

Robinson's critique of the system begins this way: "If you run an educational system based on standardization and conformity that suppresses individuality, imagination, and creativity, don't be surprised if that's what it does" (xxii).

Robinson strongly advocates for change and urges others to join him. He puts it this way: "You can be part of the change. To do that, you need three forms of understanding: a *critique* of the way things are, a *vision* of how they should be, and a *theory of change* for how to move from one to the other" (xxiv). A *vision for change*, according to Robinson, would encourage creativity and opportunities for curiosity and imagination. He adds, "Creativity draws from many powers that we all have by virtue of being human. Creativity is possible in all areas of human life, in science, the arts, mathematics, technology, cuisine, teaching, politics, business, you name it. And like many human capacities, our creative powers can be cultivated and refined" (118–119).

Robinson calls for "the change agents who can see the shape of a different future and are determined to bring it about through their own actions and by working with others." He adds, "Because when enough people move, that is a movement. And if the movement has enough energy, that is a revolution" (251).

TEACHING CREATIVE THOUGHT

Agents of change are gathering momentum, as evidenced by art educators Diane B. Jaquith and Nan E. Hathaway. They acknowledge Sir Ken Robinson and other leaders in the field as pointing the way for education in the direction of the 21st-century skills movement, which includes focusing on creativity, innovation, invention, communication, and collaboration. Acquiring these contemporary skills will be "process-oriented, not product-driven," and based on learning through discovery. As a result, "The work itself will be unique and reflect the interests and ability of the student, not the teacher" (Jaquith and Hathaway 2012, 2–3).

Art Educator Tannis Longmore's essay entitled, "Supporting Young Artists as Independent Creators" advises art teachers to be aware of the underlying messages they send. Concerned that teachers do not understand the importance of scribbling and art exploration to child development, she notes, "They may guide children to spend their time in art class assembling crafts or imitating art masters to achieve products recognizable to adults." Art teachers actually discourage creativity with activities that have predetermined outcomes; Longmore observes, "A hidden curriculum, opposite of the teacher's intention, emerges when all, or most, artistic and aesthetic direction comes from the teacher. In this unintended curriculum, creativity belongs to the teacher" (Longmore 2012, 58).

Nan Hathaway observes that "in many art classrooms expectations of conformity and compliance are every bit as prevalent as in every other class. . . . Sometimes there is little left for students to do but carry out the teacher's step-by-step art project, a rather unappealing endeavor for creative children brimming with their own ideas about what to make and how to make it!" But it does not have to be this way. Hathaway explains, "Students in a learner-directed studio setting work in a manner consistent with practicing artists—they identify ideas and problems of interest; select materials and methods; practice, perfect, and assess their work. In this design, students aren't merely learning *about* art, they are learning *through* art as they assume the role of artists" (Hathaway 2012, 84–85).

Choice-based art education is gaining momentum in the schools. Notably, educators Katherine M. Douglas and Diane B. Jaquith are among the cofounders of an educational organization: Teaching for Artistic Behavior which they have connected to choice-based education. Teaching for Artistic Behavior (TAB) is defined as "Activities that inform and sustain creative process are *artistic behaviors*. . . . These behaviors support artistic inquiry and self-driven activities for individuals during and outside of art class" (Douglas and Jaquith 2009, 2).

> Decision making resides in student hands, and this shift in control may be disorienting for art teachers. Confidence, perseverance, risk taking, and innovation are true outcomes of authentic art teaching and learning. It takes tremendous trust to allow student work to be unexpected and unknown. There is a change in outcomes that takes place when control moves from teacher to student. (Douglas and Jaquith 2009, 40)

Choice practice supports independent learning through intrinsic motivation as the children are able to move around to different art centers in the room and engage with their own choice of art materials. Children have the opportunity to learn from their peers and can decide whether to work in collaboration with others. Teachers are careful to observe, affirm effort, and call attention to discoveries made by the children. Choice-based art teachers, for instance, can assist children to overcome the fear of making an error in painting sessions. According to the authors, "When fear of mistakes is taken away, children become free with the brush and more experimental. Encourage students to practice making mistakes and then fixing them" (64).

CreatED is an educational program developed by Crayola® based on findings that "compelling evidence supports creative teaching strategies." According to Crayola's Web site, "Education researchers and thought leaders tell us that new and more effective teaching strategies infuse creativity." This infusion of creativity and the arts is across the grades and throughout the curriculum. The focus of the Crayola Education program is on "transformative change, project-based and inquiry-based learning, and creative leadership as central."

Crayola has offered funding to schools through the Champion Creatively Alive Children grants. One of the grants was awarded to an elementary school in Creedmoor, North Carolina. "According to the principal, 36 percent of students' parents don't speak English fluently and find classic school-based parent events intimidating." So "Create Night" was planned and held in a local community center. The results were "stunning, with tenfold increases in participation," rising from 15 to 150 participants. As Creedmoor teacher Stephanie Layton explained, "Life is tough here due to poverty. Only four of my 24 kindergarteners' parents have jobs. Our Create Night helped parents to see that I'm not judgmental." One of the art experiences on Create Night was a "Visions of a Child's Future" exercise. Parents and children discussed and worked on art about how creativity can shape their future. According to Layton, "The art gave me the opportunity to see parents' passions for their children. I am honored that they shared so much with me. I'm touched by how much closer we have become" (Sterman 2017, 10–11).

Libraries can serve as an important support for schools needing resources to meet the creative needs of children in the community. Schools may only be able to go so far before encountering the limitations of the system. Libraries have always provided the services that support learning objectives by offering preschool storytimes, afterschool programs, and summer reading. These services can also be extended to offer arts- and creativity-based programming that will supplement the goals of developing 21st-century creative skills.

4

Learning through Creating

CREATIVITY FROM THE START: THE REGGIO EMILIA APPROACH

The schools of Reggio Emilia are a world-renowned inspiration. These preschools began in a devastated region of Northern Italy at the end of World War II. Hope was placed in the children. The founder, Loris Malaguzzi, led the way. He was essential to the development of the Reggio Emilia approach and eventually to the expansion of its influence.

Reggio Emilia educators have not sought to create a model to be duplicated by other preschools and early childhood systems. Nevertheless, the inspiration of the Reggio approach has been widespread. This acclaim was influenced by an article in *Newsweek* magazine in the early 1990s that placed Reggio Emilia among the ten best schools in the world in the early childhood category. Through the decades, the central premises of Reggio Emilia have been extensively studied, and the philosophy has influenced many working with young children throughout the world.

Malaguzzi is known for saying that the child has *a hundred languages.* The teachers at Reggio observe and listen attentively to the children to foster communication. "Young children are encouraged to explore their environment and express themselves through all of their natural 'languages,' or modes of expression, including words, movement, drawing, painting, building, sculpture, shadow play, collage, dramatic play, and music. Leading children to surprising levels of symbolic skills and creativity" (Edwards, Gandini, and Forman 1993, 3–4).

At Reggio, a high level of creativity is not unusual. Malaguzzi maintained that "we do not consider creativity sacred, we do not consider it as extraordinary but rather as likely to emerge from daily experience. This view is now shared by many" (70).

Although this view of creativity as an everyday experience is indeed shared by many, the vast majority of our systems nevertheless cling to the belief that creativity belongs to those with rare talents. The arts are compartmentalized and kept at a distance from more "serious" academic studies.

Renowned Reggio Emilia Educator Carla Rinaldi contended, "We are too often taught to separate that which is connected, to divide rather than bring together the disciplines." She added, "For this reason, it is absolutely indispensable to reconsider our relationship with art as an essential dimension of human thinking. The art of daily life and the creativity of daily life should be the right of all" (Rinaldi 2015, 46).

Educators admit there is a long way to go before the arts are recognized as fundamental and essential. There are some progressive schools and institutions that are the exception and those, such as Reggio Emilia, are the inspiration for transformation. Howard Gardner, who is renowned for his theory of multiple intelligences, praised the Reggio community by stating, "In Reggio, the teachers know how to listen to children, how to allow them to take the initiative, and yet how to guide them in productive ways . . . Reggio successfully challenges so many false dichotomies: art vs. science, individual vs. community, child vs. adult, enjoyment vs. study, nuclear family vs. extended family; by achieving a unique harmony that spans these contrasts."

Gardner goes on to challenge our current system.

> As an American educator, I cannot help but be struck by certain paradoxes. In America we pride ourselves on being focused on children, and yet we do not pay sufficient attention to what they are actually expressing. . . . We call for artistic works, but we rarely fashion environments that can truly support and inspire them. We call for parental involvement, but are loathe to share ownership, responsibility, and credit with parents. . . . We hail the discovery method, but we do not have the confidence to allow children to follow their own noses and hunches. We call for debate, but often spurn it; we call for listening, but we prefer to talk. (Gardner 1993, xi–xii)

CREATIVE MUSEUMS

Reggio Emilia has influenced both schools and children's museums. Prominently among these museums are the Eric Carle Museum of Picture Book Art and Boston Children's Museum. The Eric Carle Museum Web site specifies, "The Art Studio at The Carle is especially inspired by Reggio

Emilia, offering guests materials and tools that encourage open-ended explorations and a chance for personal expression" (Eric Carle Museum of Picture Book Art 2018).

The Art Studio at the Boston Children's Museum was also influenced by Reggio Emilia. Bridget Matros and a colleague were hired in 2001 to create an art program at the museum. Matros wrote candidly about these experiences in an essay aptly entitled, "Handprint Turkeys and the Cotton Ball Snowman: Is There Hope for an Artful America?"

Soon after being hired by the museum, it became apparent that the system lacked basic information about art and childhood creative development. According to Matros, "Our first order of business was to reject the museum's suggestion that we facilitate themed crafts, and so we began our job of schooling the institution itself on art-for-art's-sake" (Matros 2010, 314).

Matros and her colleague established an art program at the Boston Children's Museum using the best applicable practices of Reggio combined with recommendations of other experts of creative development in psychology and education. When visitors to the museum began to come into the art studio, however, the mixed response was as surprising as it was disillusioning. Matros came to realize that most adults fear art and shun creative experiences. Although the children were often eager to participate, the adult caregivers were not. Adults hung back, protesting that they were "uncreative" and were reluctant to try art making at all. Worse yet, the adults seemed to know nothing about supporting creativity in children and would actively sabotage the process by dictating messages such as these: "Stop playing around, and make something good." Words like these prohibited creative exploration and sent false messages that implied, *Art making can be done wrong. Art making is done for the approval of others*" (320).

Matros was alarmed by her observations that the majority of adults did not understand what it means to be creative. She recognized this as a *creative deficiency* characterized by "the inability to imagine, to 'think out of the box,' or to problem solve; a censoring of self-expression, and a lack of confidence in a wide range of activities that truly cannot be done wrong." Adults with this deficiency, in turn, inflict it on children by interfering with the creative process and with "anti-art" behaviors such as "meddling, insulting, and prohibiting" (315–316).

So how did Matros and her colleague handle these challenges? They focused on reaching the *adults* by creating a place with a "basic foundation of safety." In this environment, the adult visitors would "feel relaxed, unjudged, and unpressured." This approach was reflected in the design of the art studio. The exterior was made to resemble a house with welcoming open doors. The bright interior featured "cozy" furniture and a homelike atmosphere. Secondly, visitors would be met in this way: "A smiling staff person greeting guests with a cache of low-pressure invitations and scripts that keep a step-ahead of every art-fearing or creativity-defeating behavior imaginable" (314–315).

The emphasis in the art studio was placed on developing creativity rather than art education. This meant reaching the very young child before the fears and creative deficiencies could take hold. The studio was designed with a special area for very young children where pre-art experiences were offered for scribbling, cutting paper, or finger painting. There was also special concern for reaching children who were disadvantaged and to nurture creativity as a "survival skill." But concern was also extended to all who are creatively "at-risk" (328).

Matros offers a series of tips for "creativity cultivators." These ideas include: simplification by repeatedly using the basic art materials, such as markers and crayons (and avoiding assembly crafts); allowing children to lead; placing focus on process while also respecting products; teaching parents about art and creative development through documentation; encouraging out-of-the-box ideas in order to validate imaginative thought; and asking "artful questions" that open dialogue that will benefit a child's creative confidence and also "rejuvenate your own wonder" (324–326).

LEARNING FROM CREATIVE MUSEUMS, SCHOOLS, AND LIBRARIES

The inspiration of those working in museums and schools who have courageously advocated for creativity can guide the way for libraries to do the same. It is possible to break the chain of fear that inhibits creativity. But we must admit that it is not only parents who pass down their fears of creativity to children; it can also be teachers, librarians, scout leaders, or any one of us. If we define ourselves as "uncreative," we pass this off as normal. If we say that the average adult is not creative, the hidden message for children is this: if you feel creative now, you will grow out of it.

What can be done? We can advocate not just for art, which is only one aspect, but for all of creativity. Children can grow up knowing of the vast potential, which is their birthright as creative human beings.

Librarians Laura Damon-Moore and Erinn Batykefer advocate for arts-related programs in libraries and have coauthored *The Artist's Library*. The authors also cofounded the *Library as Incubator Project*. Libraries can be excellent *creative crucibles* that the authors describe as "art-making spaces that contribute to the cultural and economic well-being of a community" (Damon-Moore and Batykefer 2014, 18).

Libraries are community microcosms. Free and open to all and well suited for reaching individuals of any age or economic background. As

Damon-Moore and Batykefer specify, "The cost of visiting certain venues, like upscale galleries and museums, can be prohibitive for students, people with lower incomes, or people with little kids. Not so at the library" (145). Libraries are "unpretentious" places to make art. This is inviting for adults who may be reluctant to take part in creative experiences elsewhere.

Inspiring ideas can be found throughout libraries. Here the arts can thrive. Many libraries are already venues for the arts with galleries, art openings, and receptions. Photography groups and aspiring writers meet in conference rooms. Community rooms in libraries can serve as venues for music, dance, theater performances, and for author readings. Damon-Moore and Batykefer quoted poet Joseph Mills: "When I walk into my library, it feels like optimism and hope. It simultaneously offers a sense of adventure and safety" (53).

"A library, to us," Damon-Moore and Batykefer reaffirmed, "is about people and skills; it's a place to connect and create." The crucial need for these places becomes increasingly apparent during an economic downturn. The authors concluded, "At a time when arts organizations and libraries are both suffering from slash-and-burn budget cuts, creating partnerships between them is a sound way to weather the storm, share resources, and work from a place of strength in the community to advocate for both libraries and arts" (155).

THE VALUE OF CREATIVE THOUGHT

Psychologist Mihaly Csikszentmihalyi has researched what makes life worth living. His extensive scientific studies have spanned over 30 years and have provided insight into what can be done to enhance the quality of life. In one of his most prominent books *Creativity: Flow and the Psychology of Discovery and Invention*, Csikszentmihalyi found that regardless of fame or fortune, creativity enhances life and enriches experience. Those who search for what is missing in life can learn from the study of those with fulfilling lives. People who express high levels of satisfaction and fulfillment often define themselves as creative individuals. After decades of research, Csikszentmihalyi reported, "The message that the creative person is sending us: You, too, can spend your life doing what you love to do . . . the love of the creative process for its own sake is available to all. It is difficult to imagine a richer life" (Csikszentmihalyi 1996, 106).

This is what we want for ourselves and for our children. But what can be done to encourage the development of creative thought? To raise creatively resourceful children, we must nurture curiosity and perseverance during the process of discovery. Motivation then comes from within to seek challenges, take risks, and persist with determination to explore creative solutions. As Csikszentmihalyi pointed out, "Problems are solved only when we devote a great deal of attention to them and in a creative way. . . . If too few opportunities for curiosity are available, if too many obstacles are placed in the way of risk and exploration, the motivation to engage in creative behavior is easily extinguished" (11). He observed that most educational systems rarely provide these opportunities. In fact, school is where curiosity and originality are most threatened with extinguishment, as evidenced by Einstein and Picasso who were among countless other creative individuals with dismal school experiences.

Why is this so? Our educational systems are a reflection of what our society values, and most value is placed on things that can be easily measured. We put a lot of stock in intelligence tests, but IQ tests cannot measure creativity or innovative thought. Opposite types of thought processes are being evaluated: *convergent* verses *divergent* thought. IQ tests evaluate *convergent* thought, which involves the ability to memorize facts and answer questions in the "right" way. This means following directions and using the correct method to solve problems that have one acceptable "right" answer. All these skills contribute to what society highly values: excellent scores in academic achievement.

Intelligence tests were designed to measure what would likely bring success in school in the 20th century, but not necessarily success in life in the 21st century. Creativity will be key. Creativity requires *divergent* thought, which Csikszentmihalyi describes in this way: "Divergent thinking leads to no agreed-upon solution. It involves fluency, or the ability to generate a great quantity of ideas; flexibility, or the ability to switch from one perspective to another; and originality in picking unusual associations of ideas. These are the dimensions of thinking that most creativity tests measure and most workshops try to enhance" (60). Great original thoughts by definition, however, will go beyond our existing systems of measurement. "Great art and great science involve a leap of imagination into a world that is different from the present . . . the whole point of art and science is to go beyond what we now consider real, and create a new reality" (63).

Howard Gardner's theory of multiple intelligences disagrees with the standard view of how intelligence is measured. He has proposed that humans have eight distinct intelligences that are uniquely configured in the individual: linguistic, logical-mathematical, musical, bodily-kinesthetic, spatial, interpersonal, intrapersonal, and naturalistic intelligence.

Gardner's theories have had far-reaching impact on traditional views of intelligence. He has endorsed three key propositions: "We are not all the same; we do not all have the same kinds of minds (that is, we are not all distinct points on a single bell curve); and education works most effectively if these differences are taken into account rather than denied or ignored."

He goes on to say, "If we ignore these differences, we are destined to perpetuate a system that caters to an elite—typically those who learn best in a certain, usually linguistic or logical-mathematical manner. On the other hand, if we take these differences seriously, each person may be able to develop his or her intellectual and social potential much more fully" (Gardner 1999, 91–92).

CREATIVITY AT THE CENTER OF INTELLIGENCE

Robert J. Sternberg placed creativity at the center of his theory of intelligence. Sternberg offered this commentary on Gardner's theory:

> Whether we agree with the theory of multiple intelligences or not, it is, I believe, fundamentally important in recognizing the multiple nature of intelligence and that theories of a single ability just do not take into account the complexity of the human mind. In my view, as a theory of single intelligence, IQ fails to do just that. My own theory attempts to go beyond IQ to understanding not just intelligence but successful intelligence in all its aspects. (Sternberg 1996, 120)

Creativity is central to successful intelligence, as Sternberg explains: "To be successfully intelligent is to think well in three different ways: analytically, creatively, and practically. Typically, only analytical intelligence is valued on tests and in the classroom. Yet the style of intelligence that schools most readily recognize as smart may well be less useful to many students in their adult lives than creative and practical intelligence" (127). In other words, a successfully intelligent person can not only *analyze* problems but also find *creative*

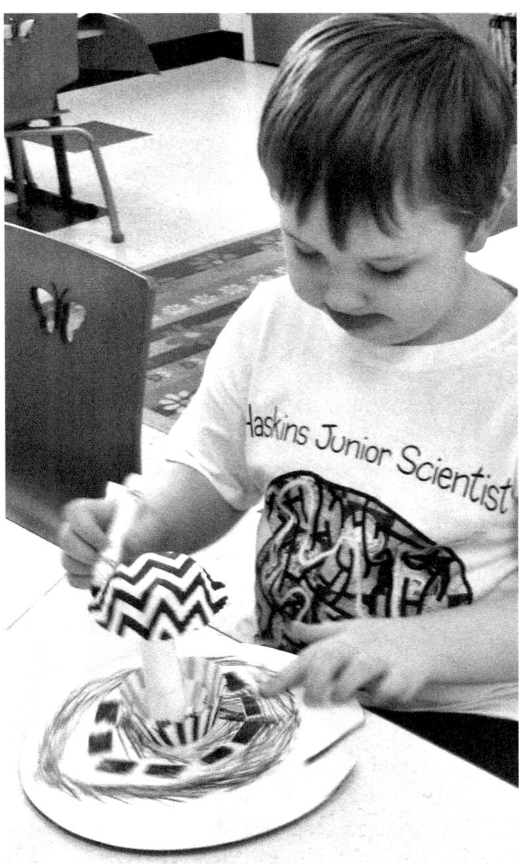

Figure 4.1   Artwork by Joseph Guarnieri-Cruess.

solutions that can be implemented in *practical* ways. Creativity, thus, serves as a bridge connecting analytical and practical intelligence. All these aspects of intelligence can be taught and continue to be enhanced through education.

Sternberg advocates for fostering creativity in schools. He takes the stance—one that sets him apart from some of the previous theorists—that young children are, indeed, creative. In both attitude and aptitude, young children have natural creativity. But the development of creative potential can be suppressed by schools that encourage "intellectual conformity." He cautions, "Children start to suppress their natural creativity when, both figuratively and literally, they are instructed to draw within the lines and are rewarded when they do so" (191). In schools, children's creative behavior may go unrecognized by teachers. Or, when children choose their own way or defy the norm, they may actually be penalized by teachers as "disruptive." Is this suppression of creativity intentional? No, according to Sternberg, "I have never met parents, teachers, or employees who believe themselves to be suppressing creativity. On the contrary, the overwhelming majority of people want to encourage creativity in others and in themselves but often are not sure of how to go about doing so" (200).

We may begin by recognizing that creative intelligence exists. We all face challenges by coming up with original thoughts and acting upon those ideas. This may be something we do far more than we realize. We are often creative.

LITERACY: LEARNING THROUGH ART

The International Reading Association (IRA) and the National Association for the Education of Young Children (NAEYC) endorse the view that art experiences enhance literacy development. The dawning of literacy begins in infancy with sound associations, language experimentation, and "reading" faces. From the earliest months of life, babies "air scribble" with their fingers, hands, and arms. These movements precede later scribbling, art making, and eventually writing. These early literacy experiences are essential. "Failure to nurture young children during these early literacy experiences may limit their reading and writing proficiency later in life" (Danko-McGhee and Slutsky 2007, 2).

Scribbling is key to acquiring skills. "Motor development, visual discrimination, cognition, creativity, social skills, and recognition of cause and effect are enhanced through scribbling experiences" (5).

"Parents and teachers should not focus on reading and writing with preschoolers (unless the child shows interest) because it may lead to failure and disrupt future literacy experiences. Early inappropriate literacy experiences may frustrate the child, leading to withdrawal from subsequent literacy experiences." The authors further counsel that copy work and coloring books are not recommended for young children. Instead, adults are encouraged to nurture scribbling that will benefit cognitive and motor development, hand-eye coordination, sequencing, as well as the visual perception and discrimination skills that will be essential for writing and reading. "Furthermore," Danko-McGhee and Slutsky specify, "these experiences do not frustrate children because they are using skills that they naturally possess, which helps to nurture their emerging passion for continuous literacy development" (9).

Literacy is usually defined as proficiency in reading and writing. Yet this is a limited view, given the vast amount of visual imagery that is ever present in education, advertisements, entertainment, and on the Internet. Literacy is decoding symbols, and the definition of literacy now needs to expand to include visual literacy, the ability to decipher and find meaning in visual images. When literacy is redefined, it becomes inclusive of many ways to communicate, as seen in the "hundred languages" of Reggio Emilia's approach through experiences with art materials. "It is imperative that adults become 'co-explorers' with the child during this important learning process" (13).

CHILDREN'S ART AT THE FOUNDATION

Susan Striker is an art educator who received Connecticut's Celebration of Excellence Award for Creativity in the Classroom. She is the author of several books, including *Please Touch* and the Anti-Coloring Book® series. She has also written *Young at Art*, a book about the value of art with toddlers and preschool-age children.

Early children's art is the foundation for reading and writing and all other skills learned later in education. Beginning around age one—just about the time that babies take their first steps—they also put their first marks on paper. The significance of early marks and scribbling as an achievement is often underestimated. As Striker pointed out, "Scribbling progressively introduces children to both the symbol recognition and production required in later reading and writing." But she laments, "Too many parents and educators think of art as decoration and are unaware of the crucial link between scribbling and writing" (Striker 2001, 5). All too often children are accused of "wasting paper" when scribbling. Nothing could be further from the truth. "Scribbling and free-drawing experiments" according to Striker, "are probably the most important art activities in which a child can engage" (7).

Susan Striker also strongly cautions parents and educators not to introduce young children to traditional art experiences, such as coloring books that require staying within the lines. Furthermore, adults should not insist that children draw recognizable objects or write letters too soon. Parents and others who dictate ideas can disrupt a child's natural process of learning through exploration. "The key words should be 'Don't teach.' Instead, *let* your child learn" (34).

Adult-pleasing tasks can divert toddlers and young children from freely scribbling, and this can be detrimental to development and creativity. "In fact, children often will interrupt their explorations to draw parent-pleasing pictures ad infinitum." Striker further explains, "Many people proudly teach their children to write their names at this time, and the children abandon scribbling to repeat these movements over and over. This should be viewed as interference of development" (26).

Also, very young children should not be required to complete "cute or clever" projects conceived by adults. As Striker cautions, "So many art projects offered by well-meaning adults that children do are so terribly 'clever' that the children who do them are overwhelmed by them. They approach the next art project with all of the inhibitions that go into making a child an underachiever" (3). Children need to focus instead on creating and developing their own ideas and abilities by using basic art materials often and repeatedly. Adults should support these child-led explorations of simple art materials rather than direct them to copy adult ideas.

THE SIGNIFICANCE OF THE SCRIBBLE

With the support of caregivers, children will begin scribbling when they are babies. At first the scribbles will appear random, but with practice they become more coordinated and controlled. Eventually children are able to make about 20 shapes that become the basis for further experimentation. Some of these shapes include dots, zigzag or wavy lines, horizontal and vertical lines, crossed lines, loops, spirals, and imperfect circles. From these early experiments comes great potential. As Striker notes, "All of the world's alphabets were derived from the shapes children experiment with as scribblers" (27).

This astonishing information about the importance of scribbling was derived from the renowned work of researcher and educator Rhoda Kellogg. Studying approximately a million children's drawings from all over the world, Kellogg developed a widely accepted system for classifying the children's art and development. She examined hundreds of thousands of children's scribbles and found that scribbles contain the beginning of all visual symbols. Most remarkably, these line elements are self-taught by the child. Kellogg discerned, "The system is logical in the sense that one sort of line formation leads to another. Whenever he uses art materials without the constraint of adult direction, the child remembers and employs as much of the system as he has taught himself" (Kellogg 2015, 51).

Kellogg documented how young children around the world have much in common in how their art skills develop. Around the age of three, children who have been free to experiment usually begin to make round or oval closed line shapes. With crossed lines over them, these shapes were thought by Kellogg to resemble a *mandala*, from the Sanskrit word for circle. According to Kellogg (65), "Mandalas are a key part of the sequence that leads from abstract work to pictorials. The child proceeds from Mandalas to Suns to Humans."

Just as no one needs to "teach" a child to walk, no one needs to teach a child how to draw a person. In fact, it is a mistake to hurry this process by an "overanxious adult." As Susan Striker contends, "This point in scribbling development is so crucial to the child's normal development that it can be devastating to now rush the process or 'teach' the child how to represent realistic objects. The capacity to discover the mandala lies within every child, as does the later need to represent people and objects realistically" (Striker 2001, 31).

Early drawings are not intended by children to be representational. It is enjoyable to freely make dots, lines, ovals, and other shapes. It is the experience that counts. With repetition, these drawings will evolve over time, to become more controlled, intentional, and purposeful. Closed shapes will be made with radiating lines that resemble the sun. Eventually, the child will draw dots and a line into the closed shape to make a face, and the radiating lines will evolve into arms and legs.

Scribbles are far from meaningless. Embedded in scribbles are the basic lines for art and for writing, and these basics are self-taught before age six. The alphabet and symbols for written language, however, will be learned from adults. Writing has always been recognized as an important achievement in literacy, but the profound connection to scribbling usually goes unrecognized. Adults often dismiss scribbles as babyish. Denigrating remarks such as, "It's just a scribble," are heard from parents and even teachers. Scribbles are thoughtlessly thrown away in front of children by adults who remember their own early art being dismissed until they could make something recognizable as having *real* meaning. Usually if early drawings were kept, they were considered cute or comical. Parents will often begin to save drawings in early elementary school that illustrate stories written by their children. Somehow, the writing legitimizes the art.

When a child is young, however, it is best to allow time for art that is freed from the need to write letters. Teaching a child to write her name and a title on drawings may tediously take over the majority of art time. Writing time and art time are best kept separate for a while, until children make the decision to write on their own drawings—if that is ever what they decide to do. Early art will continue to flow onward when freed from adult interventions. Naming everything in writing will only slow down or even halt the process altogether. An imaginative drawing that a child first describes as "a sun" may become "a spider," then "cherry pie slices" and then "a Ferris wheel." This is the height of creativity. It is best not to block this exuberant flow of ideas.

Again and again child development experts caution us not to force young children into adult-pleasing activities that will substitute for scribbling and the authentic self-guided experiences children need for early literacy and creative development.

The New York Public Library has recognized this need and reaches out with early literacy information to parents and caregivers, knowing that they are the most important teachers of young children. The *ABC Read with Me* program provides information online through the library Web site that encourages adults every day to read, talk, sing, write, play, and have fun with children while building language skills. Encouraging early literacy in writing is further described in this way: "Encourage scribbling! Keep crayons and paper on a table where your child can practice" (New York Public Library, 2018).

As children grow, more and more their art will be influenced by the world around them. About age four to seven, the size, color, and placement of objects on the paper will be random. Then around age seven, the base line may appear in their drawings. Typically, this lower line on the paper represents the ground or the floor. Children may also use another line at the top of the drawing to represent the sky. Drawings become more formulaic as children work out a system to repeatedly depict objects. Then for children between the ages of 9 and 12, the concern about realism and detail increases, as well as an increased self-consciousness about art abilities. Unfortunately, many children stop drawing at this stage of art development.

Young people need the support and encouragement of an environment conducive to creativity to open the way for art to be a bridge to literacy and to remain a means of expression throughout life.

THE BRIDGE TO LITERACY

Meredith Barnett, associate editor/writer for National Association of Elementary School Principals (NAESP) magazine, has advocated for arts-centered instruction that serves as a bridge to literacy. "A growing body of research," Barnett writes, "supports the notion that art isn't just helpful for learning, but is an essential component to it—specifically for reading" (Barnett 2013, 20). Literacy involves the vision, hearing, and language centers of the brain, and the arts activate these regions. Art can serve to build and strengthen connections, providing a bridge to deepen understanding and fluency.

Barnett points to success of arts-immersed literacy instruction. DREAM (Developing Reading Education with Arts Methods) is a grant-funded initiative that "trains California third- and fourth-grade teachers in arts/literacy practices, and after its first two years of implementation, language arts test scores of students in these teachers' classrooms increased by 87 points." Barnett also pointed to arts and literacy initiatives in the Midwest at Ridgeway Elementary School in Columbia, Missouri. Improved confidence was noted in students who had been reluctant to write in the past. Students learned how to visualize before writing by using a method called "visual thinking strategies" (21).

WHAT ARE VISUAL THINKING STRATEGIES?

Visual Thinking Strategies (VTS) is a teaching methodology that encourages children to see, think, and talk about art. It was developed by Abigail Housen, a cognitive psychologist, and Philip Yenawine, a former director of education at the Museum of Modern Art. Originally focusing on elementary-age children, this method has been extended to include younger children in preschool. By encouraging children to observe and talk about art, the VTS approach is "developing visual literacy alongside verbal literacy" (Yenawine 2018, 9). Visual literacy is facilitated through adults asking children open-ended questions that encourage close observation, critical thinking, interpretation, and expression of meaning found in art images. Children's social skills are developed through respectful listening and collaborative learning.

VTS is used in schools and art museums, including the Eric Carle Museum of Picture Book Art. It is described on their Web site in 2018 in this way: "At The Carle we use carefully selected original illustrations to engage students in facilitated discussions through the use of the VTS open-ended questions: What's going on in this picture? What do you see that makes you say that? What more can we find?" The Carle also advocates "The Whole Book Approach" developed by former museum educator, Megan Dowd Lambert. She recognizes "the picture book as an art form." Lambert, in her book *Reading Picture Books with Children*, advocates encouraging listeners in storytime to carefully observe and engage in conversation about the pictures in the book. She supports pausing during reading to provide time for "reflection, clarification, and expansion" to aid comprehension and to develop verbal and visual literacy (The Eric Carle Museum of Picture Book Art 2018).

ART-BASED LITERACY

Educator Beth Olshansky, founder of the Center for Advancement of Art-Based Literacy at the University of New Hampshire, has developed an approach to literacy learning using art to enhance reading and writing skills of school-age children in grades 1–6. Effective for learners at all levels, this art-based method has been proven to be especially effective in improving literacy skills for "reluctant" readers and writers, many of whom may be *visual* rather than *verbal* learners. Educational systems, Olshansky contends, have "a hidden verbal bias." This is the way instructions are primarily delivered—even in reading and writing. "Without intending to, we have created an educational system that tests students for a limited kind of intelligence (predominately verbal-logical)," according to Olshansky. She adds that the system then "identifies many of them as deficient (across the board and not just in this limited realm). . . . This only compounds the challenges faced by those who do not fit into our verbocentric box" (Olshansky 2008, 14).

Art is a universal language, the first written language of human beings as a species and for each of us as individuals. The significance of this should not be underestimated. Before children can write, they have abilities to "read" pictures and create pictures that can be read by others. Olshansky elaborates, "Pictures are indeed a child's first written language, and one that children generally acquire on their own. Unlike writing (letters, words, and sentences), pictures are a language that does not have to be taught" (15). These natural abilities in the language of pictures should not be dismissed as insignificant. Art can become a lifeline for those who struggle because they are not verbal learners.

Based on research and decades of experience as an educator, Olshansky developed and practiced an Artists/Writers workshop in which children study the interweaving of art and words in picture books and then create their own books. Unlike author's workshops where the writing comes first followed by the illustrations, the art comes first.

The art media the children used were primarily watercolor resist or collages made from hand-painted textured papers. The collage-inspired stories were especially notable for creative responses. Gazing at these abstract papers that were cut and pasted for collages sparked a myriad of imaginative visualizations by the children: animal shapes, night skies, lush landscapes, and underwater scenes, as well as inspired story writing with rich descriptive detail. Olshansky noted, "I observed that students who made their pictures first made the greatest advances in their writing. Their stories were far more imaginative and their writing was far richer in detail and description than stories produced by the students who chose to write first" (29).

The impact of this art-based writing improved both language skills and visual literacy, as well as significantly bolstered the children's confidence in their abilities. Olshansky's methods have been structured for educational purposes and are intended for teachers. Aspects of this approach, however, can motivate leaders of writing workshops or facilitators of art-based creativity programs in libraries to take another perspective, allowing art to empower imaginative writing.

CREATING BOOKS IN LIBRARIES

The creation of books written by children with their own original art can be a vital component for any library-based creativity program. It is simple to assemble small blank books with 8 to 10 pages using string, a booklet stapler, or a manual binding machine. Folded books can be made with origami techniques. Children delight in taking part in the construction from the beginning.

An extensive assortment of books have been illustrated and written by children in the art studio programs, including some with black pages illustrated with luminous paint markers. There have been stories about mermaids and sailors, interplanetary travel, choosing your own adventure (with multiple outcomes), and pop-up surprise books. One foldout book revealed pages of origami butterflies opening their splendid wings.

There have been many wordless books where the art tells the whole story, and a few books dense with tiny printed text describing complex tales and adventures. There have been fantasies and mysteries with dangerous turns of events threatening superheroes and treacherous villains. Other books have been filled with sly wit and silly humor.

Creating a book is undeniably where art merges with literacy. This is never more clearly evident than in the efforts of children as artists/writers. Illustration and creative writing belong together. Each enhances the other. Children are most pleased and excited—and eager to share their work with others—when they have created a little book that is genuinely their own. Some of these efforts may be saved for generations as heirlooms.

Completing a full book or several books can involve multiple sessions devoted to this purpose. But library art sessions always contend with time limitations. Focusing on creating the cover of the book can be a reasonable goal with rest of the work completed at home. Just having finished the cover art and title is quite a motivation for children to follow through on their own. If they have managed to do a few pages, then it is a cliffhanger that they are eager to resolve!

Even when not in the process of making books, children will often choose to write about their artwork, using words to elaborate on the scene.

A child draws a dragon and then writes a list of all its magical features: fire breathing, invisibility, night vision, high-flying wings. This spontaneous writing is not a distraction from the creative experience but is an extension of it. This is the art of creative writing.

As a collaborative variation, children's art-inspired poems or one-page stories could be photographed and combined into a collection or an anthology demonstrating how art and literacy interconnect in library creativity programs.

When progressive schools, museums, and libraries advocate for literacy that literally goes beyond words and into the symbolic realm of visual art, then a vast expressive potential will unfold. The inviting pages of blank books will entice original stories and imaginative works of art. With the understanding that creativity is at the center of intelligence, literacy becomes much more than reading books. Literacy becomes creating them. Libraries will become inspiring places for creative expression.

5

Creating Balance

WHY THE ART STUDIO IS A SCREEN-FREE ZONE

The digital age defines us. Global access to instantaneous information has transformed distance and time. It seems that the world, indeed the universe, is at our fingertips, just a few clicks away. It is a paradox of this age of technology and connectivity that we are at risk of becoming increasingly isolated from one another.

According to the American Academy of Pediatrics (AAP) article, "Parenting and Digital Media," "Children today average more hours engaged with media each week than they do engaged with almost any other activity (between 6 and 9 hours/day). Population-based studies have documented associations between excessive digital media use and obesity, developmental delays, and academic (or learning) difficulties." Its recommendations included: "For restrictive mediation, we advise parents to minimize screen time for young children so that they have time for the hands-on play and interactions needed for optimal development" (Coyne et al. 2017). The American Academy of Pediatrics policy statement on the use of digital media with young children has advised keeping "parent–child playtimes screen free for children and parents" (Radesky and Christakis 2016).

The art studio has been designated as a screen-free zone. Signs are placed around the room advising to disconnect from tech and connect with one another. It became apparent years ago that these signs were necessary. When the Open Art Studio program first began at the library, caregivers frequently attempted to "drop off" their young children. Once these adults were persuaded to stay, some gave little or no attention to their child or what was happening in the room. Standing behind the children working at the art table, a few adults texted and scrolled through their phones. Soon others took this as their cue to do the same; it wasn't long before the majority of adults in the room were on their phones. The result was a room divided.

Most children submissively accepted this and worked quietly with little or no interaction with their caregivers. But a few wanted attention. When children asked for it, adults often took this as an interruption. As a result, some children became increasingly needy, and their whining pleas only heightened the impatience of caregivers. A few children tried mischief to gain attention, such as intentionally nudging art materials off the table. Repeated behaviors like this led adults to suggest leaving the art studio. This was the last thing the children wanted and so the tears began.

It soon became obvious that this was no way to run an art program. Learning from these early mistakes, we made signs that clearly marked the room as a "screen-free zone" and invited adults to take part in the art experience. It took a while before the full effect was felt, but eventually adults began to eagerly accept our request. Instead of standing behind children and texting, the caregivers came in and straightaway sat down next to the child. Instead of only glancing at the child's completed artwork, the adults were aware during the process of what the child was creating. Best of all, the adults now became engaged in making their own artwork. And the children knew that someone who cared was right there by their side, someone who could respond at a moment's notice. As a result, children worked more independently. There was no need to beg for attention. There was nothing to interrupt. They were sharing a parallel experience. They each could go at their own pace together.

LEARNING FROM EXPERTS

The consequences of technology distraction impact both child and parent, according to Julia Cameron, a best-selling author on creativity. Writing on how to raise creative children, she observed, "We miss something—and withhold something from them—if we are buried in our phone, deleting spam or surfing the Internet. The advent of the smartphone becoming the 'world in our pocket' is both a blessing and a curse. We must be very conscious of how we use this tool. Anytime we are distracted by it unconsciously, we are telling our children that something behind that screen has priority over them—and we are teaching them to focus on screens themselves" (Cameron and Lively 2013, 177).

As psychologist Rollo May asserted, "The danger always exists that our technology will serve as a buffer between us and nature, a block between us and the deeper dimensions of our own experience" (May 1975, 67).

Clinical Psychologist Catherine Steiner-Adair, an instructor at Harvard Medical School, is concerned about children born and raised in this digital age and the real experiences and encounters that are being displaced. "The rich complexities of imagination and sensory, social, and emotional interactions . . . go far beyond the simple hunt-and-tap experience of the digital environment," she observes in her insightful book, *The Big Disconnect* (101–102).

"Lost is the slow-paced hands-on practice that develops small motor skills, dexterity, and eye-hand coordination. The sensory experience that goes with that—the touch and smell and messy fun of play—is gone, too" (86). Steiner-Adair concludes, "Our challenge as technology continues to open new worlds of possibility is to not let new opportunities and new apps obliterate old truths. Children need our attention . . . and we can teach our children how to be in this new world. There we can deepen connections, cultivate closeness, and push *pause* more often to savor the gift of time" (295).

Open Art Studio groups bring families together to encounter essential experiences that have often been undervalued, displaced, or even lost in our hurried tech-driven world. No virtual art experience gives little hands the feeling of rolling and forming warm clay. Only firsthand experience can teach little fingers how to crisply snip paper with scissors. Children need to learn how to manage the fascinating stickiness of wet glue before learning to cut and paste on a screen. A digital paintbrush cannot compare to real paint lavished on a brush spreading delight to the full height and distance of a reach. There are no substitutes for real experiences.

A child's imagination should not be limited by a screen. Children will act out all sorts of fantasy scenarios in their play and in their artwork, too. All this heroism or villainy normally involves some pretend violence. This can be a way for children to gain power over their fears. But violent virtual games do not come from the minds of children. Pediatrician Edmond Schoorel cautions us thus: "Real play is guided by children's imaginations; virtual games are guided by their designer's imagination" (Schoorel 2016, 102). The images and fantasies conjured by an adult mind are very different from what a child would conceive. Schoorel identifies video games as an *anti-encounter.*

This stands in sharp contrast to a creative experience. As psychologist Rollo May explains, "The first thing we notice in a creative act is that it is an *encounter.* Artists encounter the landscape they propose to paint. . . . They are, as we say, absorbed in it. Or, in the case of abstract painters, the encounter may be with an idea, an inner vision. . . . The paint, the canvas, and the other materials then become a secondary part of this encounter; they are the language of it, the *media,* as we rightly put it." Rollo May goes on to explain, *"Escapist creativity is that which lacks encounter"* (May 1975, 34–35).

Schoorel is one of many pediatricians who is concerned about not only the content of video games for children but also the massive amount of time that is consumed playing them. When this amount of time is excessive, it invariably displaces other experiences: real experiences. During this time, these children are not on the swings at playground or playing ball with the neighbors down the street. They are not making mud pies in their own backyards. More and more children spend their leisure time inside and in front of screens. These virtual experiences on "cyberplaygrounds" have taken them in, literally.

The real places where children were once free to roam, the outside domain of children, has shrunken ever smaller with each generation. Compared to where children's parents and great-grandparents were able to travel on their own, today's children are in confinement. Children of generations past rode bikes to the playground, walked to neighborhood stores, and chased fireflies long after dark. Some still do, but now the zone of independence is much smaller, and it may continue to diminish. Just walk down any neighborhood street at dusk in the summertime; home after home will glow with the light of screens. There are large screens on the walls and smaller screens on the desks. This is often where the children play now.

Many well-meaning parents and teachers are over-scheduling children, and the remaining free time is consumed by electronic devices that displace spontaneous play and the chance for real interaction with others. Families go to libraries to sit down in front of screens, and the children play computer games for hours. They come home and scatter to separate rooms, where the waiting screens light up. Even at the dinner table, heads are bowed over phones. Whole families dine out this way, each with their own diversion in hand and no interaction at all. Much of technology use is isolating, especially when each person is literally left to their own devices.

Neuroscientist Susan Greenfield in her book *Mind Change* asserts, "Creative thinking cannot be purchased, downloaded, or guaranteed, but it can be fostered with the right environment" (Greenfield 2015, 246). When we are in our own imaginative world, the ideas are our own. We guide the way. We are the driver. But Greenfield explains that when we enter into a cyber world, "the screen can be the driver . . . spectacular cyberexperiences contrived by someone else engulf you. You are now a passive recipient, and even though games . . . allow you to modify and create worlds, it is always within the secondhand parameters of the game designer's thinking." With frequent gaming, real experiences will be displaced. Real-life activities, according to Greenfield, will be "forfeited in favor of a cyberactivity." This is a *less* active environment, "where taste, smell, and touch are not stimulated, where we can be completely sedentary for long periods of time, yet where the ensuing experience trumps more traditional ways of life for appeal and excitement" (22–23).

This is a seductive world. We are less active and interactive with others, yet we are rewarded for this. With very little effort, click, click, click, or with the touch of a screen, we have far reaching information at our fingertips, or we can be transported into realms beyond our imagining. Is this educational and enriching? Yes, it absolutely can be. But it can be impoverishing too, especially for children who spend most of their time gaming there. Excessive absorption in a two-dimensional world means that they are disengaging in the three-dimensional world around them.

Experts agree that finding balance is key.

EXPERTS ON LIMITING TECH

Steve Jobs once said, "I've helped with more computers in more schools than anyone else in the world and I'm absolutely convinced that is by no means the most important thing. The most important thing is a *person*. A person who incites and feeds your curiosity; and machines cannot do that in the same way that people can" (Jobs 2011, 55).

It may be surprising to learn that when Steve Jobs was the CEO of Apple, he kept technology to a minimum with his children. Journalist Nick Bilton of the *New York Times* in 2010 asked Jobs if his kids loved the newly introduced iPad. Jobs unexpectedly responded, "They haven't used it. . . . We limit how much technology our kids use at home." Amazed by this, Bilton then went on to interview other prominent executives in technology and learned they also placed strict limits on screen time for their children. From this he concluded that these tech C.E.O.s "seem to know something that the rest of us don't." Among the dangers cited were: "Exposure to harmful content like pornography, bullying from other kids, and perhaps worse of all, becoming addicted to their devices, just like their parents." As a result, content was monitored, and time on devices was often strictly limited. Schoolwork and homework were the exceptions. Another notable exception was offered in an interview with Ali Partovi, a founder of iLike and advisor to Facebook, who said, "Just as I wouldn't dream of limiting how much time a kid can spend with her paintbrushes . . . I think it's absurd to limit her time spent creating computer art."

Writing an article in *Business Insider*, Chris Weller states, "Interviews with Bill Gates, Steve Jobs, and other tech elites consistently reveal that

Silicon Valley parents are strict about technology use." This should be seen as a red flag for all of us. Even the former CEO of Microsoft, Bill Gates, placed limits on screen time, and he also did not let his children have cell phones before age 14.

Amy Fleming wrote an article for *The Guardian* entitled, "Screen Time v Play Time: What Tech Leaders Won't Let Their Own Kids Do." Fleming interviewed parents in high-tech leadership positions in the United Kingdom and the United States on how much tech is too much for children. Among those interviewed was Pierre Laurent, a former marketing manager at Microsoft and Intel, who was then working on a Silicon startup. Before age 12, his children were not exposed to screens—TV, computers, or smartphones. Laurent first became wary of the "hooking effect" of screens while working at Intel. The intent is to keep the screen user's attention from wandering off. Laurent asserted, "It looks like it's soothing your child and keeping them busy so you can do something else, but that effect is not very good for small children." He maintained, "It stops them discovering the world with their senses."

Fleming also interviewed Karim Dia Toubajie, an interaction designer for Songkick, who previously worked for PlayStation. He stated, "I'm conscious of how easy it might be for children to get obsessed with digital. Working in technology, I'm also aware how these channels are designed for continual user journeys, with no defined end point . . . to be addictive" (Fleming 2015).

BALANCING TECHNOLOGY WITH CREATIVITY

Leaders in technology know that being tech savvy also means being smart about tech. If you do not control it, it can control you. Tech should not displace real-world encounters, because it can become all-consuming—addictive—especially if given too much and too soon to children. It is misguided to use tech as a digital pacifier that keeps children quiet and occupied. Unfortunately, it works all too well. Lively children will soon learn to sit submissively and stare at a flat screen, one that "screens" out the surrounding world. For hours they will dutifully dress virtual paper dolls, color with virtual crayons, accumulate stuff to build and defend worlds, or destroy aliens before they are destroyed. They sit and stare and click. Stare and click. They do not run or walk or talk. They sit pacified for hours. But what activity would they have done? Where would they have explored? What thoughts, ideas, and magical fantasies would have been acted out? What would they have created from their *own* imaginations?

In their book *Wired to Create*, researchers Kaufman and Gregoire further caution us all about the impact of tech distraction. We pay a price for constantly disrupting our own attention. The authors' research revealed, "Resisting the siren song of digital distractions can be incredibly difficult, but our creative capacity may depend on our ability to do so. Insofar as we succumb to distraction, our ability to access that mental space where our richest ideas and visions live is compromised—and so is our ability to connect deeply with what's *outside* of us" (Kaufman and Gregoire 2015, 110).

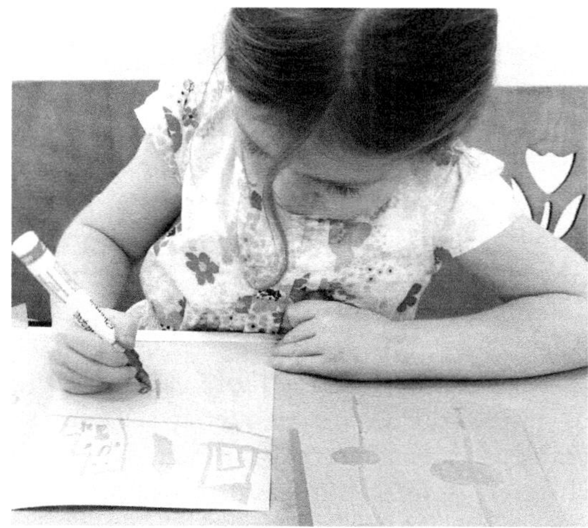

Figure 5.1   Creating in the library art studio.

Parents looking for books for their children in libraries have confided, "I want my child to spend *less* time on the computer and less time watching TV. How do I get them to shut it all off? How do I limit screen time?" What is the answer? The vast majority of experts agree that it is important to place limits on tech and screen time. But simply insisting on disconnecting will be counterproductive if nothing takes the place of these experiences. Time limits may actually worsen the problem and increase cravings for the stimulation of tech when access is abruptly lost.

The key is to *diversify* and *expand* rather than *limit* children's experiences and to provide enticing alternatives and experiential learning. Libraries can balance virtual experiences with real encounters. Libraries can also lead the way in offering families a chance to become involved in hands-on art experiences and to take part in creative collaboration. When everyday creative experiences become a priority at home, there will be plenty of time for playing together and interaction. There will be time for making music, dancing around, acting out stories, and pretending. The imaginative possibilities will open up when sitting down at a creativity table. Time away from tech will also give more time for quiet thought, reading, relaxing, and venturing outside.

Author Richard Louv, in his book *Last Child in the Woods*, is concerned by children's lack of connection with the natural world. He puts it this way: "Not that long ago, the sound track of a young person's days and nights was composed largely of the notes of nature. . . . Today, the life of the senses is, literally, electrified" (Louv 2005, 56). He quotes one fourth-grader as saying, "I like to play indoors better, 'cause that's where all the electrical outlets are" (10).

As we all know, we do not need outlets anymore. Tech can go with us on a hike up a mountain or on a walk down city sidewalks. When people step off curbs into streets with their awareness narrowed down to a handheld screen, they are not where they are. This disconnection from the here and now is dangerous and is cause for deep concern. Catherine Steiner-Adair put it this way: "Based on studies of highway accidents involving drivers who were texting and reports of pedestrians injured while reading or texting, we know that the distraction factor is real and significant, even when our life and the lives of others depend on our staying focused" (Steiner-Adair and Barker 2014, 59).

How can we become more engaged in the here and now? How can we become more aware of our surroundings—our environment—and help children to do the same? We begin by recognizing that the world of today's children is often significantly different from that of their parents and grandparents. While the virtual world has been expanding, the world of real encounters may have diminished in many ways.

Local woods and open fields have been disappearing from the neighborhoods where previous generations played as children. Richard Louv describes this as the "new landscape of childhood" (11). In the name of progress, many forests and fields were "developed" into suburban housing, business courts, and shopping malls. Even where they still exist, these areas are not where the children are found. Children are inside. Louv states, "One price of progress is seldom mentioned: a diminished life of the senses. . . . Twenty-first century Western culture accepts the view that because of omnipresent technology we are awash in data. But in this information age, vital information is missing. Nature is about smelling, hearing, tasting, seeing . . . awakening to nature's sensory gift . . . wisdom and wonder" (57).

Louv believes that there is hope. He recommends many ways to deepen the attachment of children with the natural environment. This includes taking along the drawing materials and paintbrushes on outside adventures. Children can then choose to record their observations of leaves, insects, and clouds. He encourages discovering special places with children and adds this advice: "Look for the edges between habitats: where the trees stop and a field begins; where rocks and earth meet water. Life is always at the edges" (172).

ENCOUNTERS WITH ART AND NATURE

How can the creative edge connect children and nature through art? The most obvious way is to venture outside. Artists throughout time created in the midst of the natural world. The method of painting *en plein air* to capture natural light used by impressionists still remains a primary mode for many contemporary artists. It is not necessary, however, to be outside in order to be aware of nature. The view from a window of a single tree can be endlessly inspiring through the seasons. Leaves will unfurl, branches will stir in a summer storm, autumn leaves will flash illumination and then drop away, and twigs will shimmer with a dusting of snow.

Bringing objects into the art studio such as leaves, pinecones, rocks, and feathers will inspire deep observation and a more profound appreciation of nature through art. These experiences should not be limited to older children, teens, and adults. Younger children can be quite interested in drawing from nature, too. When they choose to draw from their observations, children become vividly aware of shapes, colors, and intricate details of natural objects. They can, for example, learn to identify trees through their leaves. One autumn leaf is pointy and red, while another is rounded and yellow. They notice textures and raised veins on the surface. Such experiences heighten a child's sense of joy and wonder while sharpening visual acuity and the ability to discern similarities and differences. Drawing from observation also refines hand-eye coordination and prewriting skills.

If an art experience has this much merit, why not do it all the time? Indeed, why not? Drawing, painting, and sculpting based on observation of objects from nature should always be an option in an art studio. It is an excellent idea to have a designated place (or many places) where these objects from nature can be found and books about the natural world can be explored.

It is best, however, to leave drawing from observations as an option, rather than requiring this experience for anyone. This is especially true for young children who need to scribble, draw freely, play, explore, and experiment at their own pace long before they will choose to draw from observation. Open art is about providing choices and not hurrying or urging children to move on to any experience before their time. Drawing directly from nature and natural objects can be an option among many possibilities. This does not rule out drawing from memory, imagination, or simply experimenting with what types of marks are made by various art materials.

A WALK THROUGH OPEN ART STUDIO

Now it is time to take a deeper look into a working art studio. Before the description of the art programs that take place there, it may be helpful to visualize the context. When a visitor to the Avon Free Public Library approaches the art studio through the children's room, they first see the lighted art gallery that resembles a village storefront. A wooden shingle roof slants above glass windows. Inside the narrow gallery is a display of photos illuminated by track lighting against a dark wall. The photos are of artwork made in the studio: scribbles to sculptures, collage to clay figures, paint pens to pastels, and illustrated book covers to painted masks. Mobiles are hung from the gallery ceiling, and clay sculptures are exhibited on low pedestals.

Passersby stop to point at the display or to read the flyers for the next series of studio sessions. To the left of the gallery, windowed doors open to the art studio. Above the entryway is an old-fashioned porch dormer in keeping with the ambience of a small village. The doors to the studio are wide open when in session. The main door is boldly painted purple. Beside it is a charming little red door just the right size for small children to enter.

Once over the threshold, the message is clear. Open Art Studio is a place for creativity. Immediately to the right is a mural of children holding hands. To the left are drying racks crowded with recent artwork. Bold geometric tiles pattern the floor. Straight ahead is a long table where people are busy making art. A grandfather sits next to a young boy, a young mother sits between twin daughters. There is a giggling group of elementary-age children with their parents and a small group of teen friends seated side by side. At a long table, everyone works together in fading afternoon light.

Just beyond this table, a narrow vertical window—nearly floor to ceiling—seems to extend the room out into the trees beyond. Suspended from the ceiling is a mobile, and baby carriage is under it. While her mother and twin sisters work at the art table, the baby is fascinated by the movement of the mobile. Balanced on wires, a school of semitransparent fish flicker in the sunlight, showing painted details as they swim slowly through currents of air. In the middle of the room, another ceiling mobile stirs delicately while balancing opaque segments of collage.

Tall windows and high ceilings in the studio create an atmosphere that is light and airy. The far walls are painted soft ivory. There is comfortable furniture, a yellow upholstered armchair, storage ottoman, floor pillows, and white bead board cabinets that seem to be from a country home rather than within a public building. Next to the wooden closet doors are low pine shelves stacked with illustrated children's stories and timeworn books on art and nature. A velveteen rabbit and a few puppets nestle among the books. In a corner are two sinks. One is at counter height and the other is much lower, just the right height for young children to wash their hands.

On the far wall is a large half-arched window. This wall is painted deep blue and has a floor-to-ceiling tree mural with a spectrum of leaves made from the cutout tracings of countless hands on paper. The blue wall appears to be the sky behind the branches of this "Tree of Diversity."

As the afternoon goes on, the art studio fills with people and becomes increasingly charged with sounds of activity. Voices in several languages lift enthusiastically over the distant notes of chamber music on the old stereo system. A few standing children are deciding where to sit down next. There are a total of four tables to choose from in the room, and each one has a group doing something else. Everyone at the main table is working with clay. At a second table, children are drawing with markers. There are drawings of trucks, scribbles, houses, pets, and fairies. One boy has folded a paper airplane, and he is adding designs to the wings. Nearby is a third table that is smaller and lower. Here a younger group is enthusiastically dotting with dot markers while their amused parents look on. On the fourth and lowest table (a round wooden old coffee table), a toddler stands and scribbles vigorously on the paper with a large diamond-shaped crayon, while her older sibling kneels nearby, rubbing leaf textures. A young boy close by is playing on a light table, stacking geometric cubes that periodically clatter down to the tiled floor to be picked up and stacked again and again.

When Open Art Studio is this busy, there can be 30 to 40 people in the room. At these times, it is recommended that two staff members facilitate creativity. Each will be responsible to observe and be alert to what is needed. One facilitator may be greeting and explaining the choices of art experiences to newcomers, while resetting the clay on the main table in the places that have recently become available. The other facilitator may be walking and observing the other side of the room, answering questions, supplying paper, and saying goodbye to families who are leaving. During these times, the pace will be rapid and swiftly changing. At other times, the art studio will become quiet with just a few children and caregivers concentrating on their independent work. Then only one staff member will be needed to monitor the room.

BEING WATCHFUL

It is relatively commonplace in busy public places, such as shopping malls, amusement parks, playgrounds, children's museums, and libraries, that young children will sometimes have inattentive or distracted caregivers. So how do we deal with these issues when they arise? Foremost, we need to be absolutely clear that safety comes first. Very young children need constant supervision. Keep the public aware of this by placing prominent signs around the room stating this: "Caregivers, Please Be Watchful at All Times." If an art material is not for children under the age of three, state this openly with signs warning about choking hazards. Also, signs on the door and elsewhere in the room remind caregivers that messiness is to be expected with art; offer the advice to "dress for mess."

Young children in Open Art Studio are encouraged to work as independently as possible, but caregivers need to be responsive to their child's needs. This means not being absorbed by a phone or a laptop. Signs notifying them that the art studio is a "screen-free zone" designate this as a place for adults to connect with their children and with the art process. Place a sign encouraging adults to participate in the art experience, especially if this is a drop-in program. The invitation that "art is for everyone" keeps the caregiver nearby and engaged in a parallel creative experience while still being responsive to the young child.

EARLY ART

The Early Art groups at the Avon Free Public Library were designed by creativity facilitator Megan Grosch. Based on her experience in Open Art Studio as a co-facilitator, she created the Early Art groups to meet the specific developmental needs of children ages two and three. Initially, it was surprising that the library would offer art sessions for children this young. But these groups intently focus on enjoying and practicing the early art and pre-literacy skills that are emerging at this stage of development. Caregivers experience firsthand how to nurture creativity from the beginning and share the delight of discovery with their children.

What a fun way to learn! There is a spirit of play that emboldens these little explorers to venture into art with caregivers by their side. Everyone is invited to learn through the joyful exploration of art materials. Adults learn too. They come to understand process art through firsthand experience. As a result, caregivers let go of the need to direct the way and allow children to make their own choices. Adults learn not to give directions for young children to make "something," such as recognizable shapes, draw pictures, or write letters of the alphabet, which would be detrimental for both development and creativity at this early age. Because most adults are not aware of the significance of scribbling and free drawing to the development of art and literacy skills, there is a need to educate parents and caregivers on these subjects.

Informational pamphlets are provided to caregivers in Early Art groups on the role of art and creativity in child development as well as the association of art to literacy. These pamphlets compiled by the library staff give a brief overview of the basic concepts, approach, and objectives of art-based creative experiences with children: "Encourage Creativity: How to Talk with Children about Their Art" and "The Creativity Center: Designing a Space to Create at Home."

Attendance in Early Art groups is kept to about 10 children with their caregivers, so it would be about 20 participants in all. The art materials are chosen to meet the developmental needs and motor skills of small children. Some crayons provided are designed with egg or geometric shapes for the grip of toddlers to fit the palm. Very large unwrapped crayons are also available. Paper provided for free scribbling is 11" × 17" or larger. At times the entire surface of the table would be covered with paper. A standing toddler making art needs a low surface (about 15 inches, or approximately the height of a coffee table).

There are small chairs at other low tables set with dot markers, washable broad-tip markers, or large colored pencils. Children can have the choice to come and go from these tables during the session, and they gleefully lead the way to each of these stations with their caregivers following them.

The longest art table has the main experience of the day and is set with either drawing or painting or collage materials. Collage has many variations. Young children have a seemingly inherent sense of beauty and composition and strong opinions about what goes where. Collage is a natural choice for young artists. Selected geometric or remnant shapes from brightly colored cardstock are boldly eye-catching when placed on white or black backgrounds. Young children are fascinated by collages with a limited palette of colors, such as white and black shapes on red paper, giving a striking high contrast effect. Larger cut shapes are easier for little fingers to pick up, and sturdy cardstock is managed much better than fragile tissue shapes. So cardstock is recommended for beginning collage experiences. Although paste or glue may be used, small glue sticks work just fine when gripped and applied by little hands.

The mysterious qualities of glue will be an ongoing adventure—often one of trial and error—for these little explorers. Purple disappearing glue may be helpful to see where the glue has landed, especially in early art experiences. But some older children will care that the glue does not entirely disappear when it dries, so clear drying glue will be preferable for them. The question of where to put the glue and how much is needed is an ongoing curiosity for little children. Under and overdoing glue is a rite of passage for these explorations. So is gluing on the wrong side and sticking things to your hands!

Intuitive adults and facilitators of creativity offer gentle guidance, assistance, or reassurance when needed. This responsiveness will serve to strengthen a child's ability to ask for help and speak up for future needs. Usually, what is needed is quite simple. For example, a little guidance on how to take off a cap or how to twist up more glue. A child may need a wet towelette to wipe or a quick trip to the sink for a wash before returning to the artwork.

When adults offer too much assistance or intervene too often without being asked, it will hinder rather than help. The motivation for this may result from adult anxieties about messiness rather than be for the sake of the child. We all know a better, faster, and easier way. But if a child has not asked for help, and seems fine dealing with little setbacks, then this is a great opportunity to gain independence and self-reliance by facing a challenge. Why else do little ones this age so often insist "I want to do it all by *myself!*"

These children are just beginning to declare their independence by saying no to adult controls. By being too critical or too helpful, adults risk taking the love of learning away. Children yearn to teach themselves and to own an accomplishment by saying, *"I did it!"* They will remember it with satisfaction and pride and retain the information longer if it was gained through their own victory. Not much will come from adult lectures on how to do everything "right" the first time. Trust that with a chance to be inquisitive, satisfy their own curiosity, and try different methods to solve problems, these children will naturally learn by teaching themselves.

Early Art is designed to be child-led through the wonders, mysteries, and revelations of these exhilarating new experiences. Young children are intrigued by the seemingly magical quality of art to make something appear that was not there before. When adults take the role of supporting art exploration, children have the choice to pursue their own ideas. Rather than doing art for the child or directing what the child will do, caregivers are requested to model creative exploration with their own art materials. This way, adults have as much fun as the children, sometimes even more!

Art is a wonderful way to learn! There is so much to enjoy in the art studio! Everyone can have fun trying easy application materials such as oil pastels, slick gel crayons, or tempera paint sticks on different colors of paper. These Early Art sessions introduce new art experiences or give a chance to gain practice with more familiar materials, such as paint. But even experienced children of this young age may have painted only a few times before. When a child is hesitant to begin, the facilitator keeps it elemental and easy: "Just try to put some color on your brush . . . now put the brush on the paper . . . practice making marks . . . move the color around on the paper . . . explore!" Simply learning how it feels to hold a paintbrush and make marks on paper can be thrilling for a very young child!

Children this age are enchanted by the simple act of painting and so it is best to keep it basic. Painting can easily be introduced one color at a time. A single color of liquid tempera will be fascinating. The low, translucent lids of no-spill cups are ideal for placing liquid paint that can be easily accessed with a brush. Begin with high contrast, such as black paint on white paper. Also, try painting with white liquid tempera on black paper for the reverse effect. In later sessions, two choices of liquid tempera—such as white and black—can be placed side by side in one shallow lid to see what happens when they are mixed together.

Initial painting sessions can also start with just a single tempera block of color. For instance, children can paint with blue on 6" × 6" squares of watercolor paper and make many of them! At first just one color at a time will be quite sufficient for little ones who are endlessly intrigued by what happens when they put water on a brush, load it up with color, then make a painting! In later sessions, other colors can be introduced one by one. Then offer two colors that can be combined. Red and yellow will yield the thrilling discovery of orange! Also, in addition to painting on the squares of watercolor paper, try offering a variety of other large geometric cut shapes: circles, triangles, and hexagons. Occasionally, there can be nature-inspired cut shapes to be painted, such as butterflies, birds, flowers, or leaf forms.

Nothing, of course, ever needs to be finished or taken home. In fact, most of the painted items in Early Art can be left behind on the drying rack, evidence that the experience of making has been enough. It is a good policy, however, to hold onto these works for a few weeks to be certain that they will not be claimed. These papers can be retained for later use for future collages and other artwork.

Caregiver response to Early Art has been enthusiastic. Grown-ups have as much fun as their little ones! They learn the value of providing creative opportunities for their children and how to joyfully take part in these experiences.

6

Facilitating Creativity

TALKING *WITH* CHILDREN ABOUT THEIR ART

Here is the moment. A child eagerly lifts up his artwork in joyful anticipation of your response. It is an exuberant painting! What do you say?

This child is giving you the honor of sharing a triumph. So take time to give all your attention. Go to the child's level to look carefully at the artwork and make direct eye contact with him. Give a glowing smile and a nod, affirming that you share in his delight. The best remarks are kept simple and value the child's choices, effort, and experience of the process.

Listening is the most important aspect of the conversation. It is easy to say too much. We all have done it. When in doubt, talk less and listen more. The best questions are left open-ended. "Please tell me more about this." Try to never impose your own ideas on the child. Everyone has made the mistake of guessing (by assuming) that what a child has created is a recognizable form.

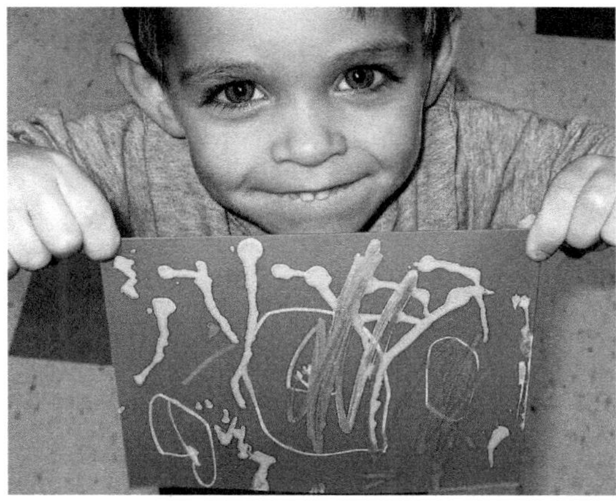

Figure 6.1   Artwork by Dylan.

75

"Oh! You have painted some green snakes!" Only to hear the frustrated response, "No." Even when we are very sure of what we are seeing, it is best not to make assumptions. Children's representational work can be elusive to the adult eye.

When someone asks, "What is *THAT*?" the child feels compelled to justify what they have been doing by giving a name to it. When the art was playful exploration, there will not be a title or theme. Nevertheless, adults often insist on an explanation. The message is that art has to *be* something. It has to be a symbol for something else, such as a tree, or it is meaningless and unimportant. This is obviously untrue. It is extremely important for adults to convey respect for children's nonrepresentational work.

Many adult caregivers will try to control the child's art process. Although well intentioned, this mistake comes from the common misperception that young children require instruction in art. When a hovering adult dictates ideas for the child and directs the "right and wrong" way to do them, it is typically under the guise of teaching art. What may actually be learned by the child is that he or she is incompetent and incapable of making independent choices. When adults try to take everything over from the onset, any creative thought on the part of the child is perceived as resistance.

A classic example would go something like this: "Why don't you paint a pretty picture for grandma? Here, just paint a square and a triangle on top to make her house . . . Oh no, that's not the right color for her house! Use yellow . . . good! Now where's the door? Why are you putting it over there? Here, let me show you . . . the door goes here! Now, do some pretty flowers in her garden . . . Wait! The *flowers* aren't green. You have all these nice colors. Use different ones for the flowers. Oh no, the colors are getting muddy. You're just making a mess . . . Stop, and go wash your hands . . . OK, now let's write 'I Love You, Grandma' on the top. How do you make an *I*? OK, now leave a little space and make the *L* . . . that's not *L*; it's backward! Not like that, like this."

Needless to say, such an experience is fraught with frustration, especially for the child. It is also apparent that grandma will not be getting a heartfelt work of art. Why are children's creative choices so often discouraged by well-meaning adults? At the core, there is a basic lack of understanding of how children learn and the importance of creativity for child development. As adults, we need to let go of the assumption that we must lead the way or children will become lost. Adults will often talk *to* children rather than *with* them. We can all learn to listen more intently to children. Responsive listening means not imposing our own ideas.

Adults must unlearn that children need constant instruction or they will fall behind. Relentless and overbearing teaching can extinguish the love of learning and crush creativity. As creativity facilitators, we need to keep this in the forefront of our thoughts. Once understood, it is easy to forget. Yet, we set the tone. We know that children learn best when they are motivated by their own curiosity and take the initiative to follow their interests. This also true of adults.

From the beginning, a facilitator invites everyone to work on their own art. As adults become invested following their own ideas, the children are freed from following constant instructions.

GOING BEYOND WORDS

Art explorations are full of wonders and discoveries that go beyond words. Taking part in this process can be more than enough. Is it really necessary that the child *talk* about the artwork at all? Maybe not. Try to be especially mindful of this while the child is still working. Talking can be an annoying interruption that interferes with concentration. Observe silences reverently.

One of the most eloquent descriptions of how to "be present" with children in a group was written by Reggio Emilia's Lella Gandini, who was observing teacher Amelia Gambetti at La Villetta School in Italy: "Amelia is able to be completely present, observing, and listening, mostly silent and alert; she becomes cognizant of what is around, what is missing, and seeks to provide or suggest what is needed." Such a presence creates "reciprocal trust with the children"(Gandini 2015, 25).

Facilitators of creativity should aspire to be present in this way. There are ways to be "silent and alert" and to convey respect that goes beyond words. Much support can be conveyed wordlessly through our facial expressions. A reassuring smile and a nod will encourage an artist to persevere through a lengthy task. A look of surprise and wonderment at an unexpected turn in the artwork will send the message that we are aware and appreciative of the process. Deep interest will be most apparent when we take the time to look intently at the artwork, especially when it's offered up for our eyes. To be specifically sought out to be shown artwork is an honor. Our reaction has been requested and will be valued. Our response can further validate that the creative process is meaningful and deepen the experience. Body language, gestures, and expressions convey much more than we ever realize.

To value art making is to value the child. In our attempt to value the process, it is important not to undervalue the product. Art is thought and feelings made visible. A finished art product is constructed from individual ideas and personal effort, and it belongs personally to the child. It is property. Children actually own very little and so their artwork is very important property indeed. It is disrespectful to ever make a mark on a child's work or to handle it carelessly. Before touching artwork, always ask the child's permission first. The rest can be conveyed wordlessly. Hold it carefully, look at it intently, and place the artwork down gently in a safe place. Carelessly folding or stacking wet artwork will ruin it. If work needs to be transported to a drying rack, it is best to have the child take it to where it will be placed. This is the quickest way to find it later. At all times, the child should be in control of what happens to the artwork and know exactly where it is placed after completion.

LISTENING RESPONSIVELY AND SPEAKING RESPECTFULLY

Given a chance, many children are effusive about their ideas and more than eager to express them. Young children who thrive on attention will initiate conversations by saying, "Look at mine!" When you are the one chosen to share the excitement of an accomplishment, it calls for a joyful response that conveys your enthusiasm: "Oh! You painted this! You mixed blue and yellow . . . Tell me what happened next. . . " If the child delights in your continued interest, feel free to continue to ask more open-ended questions, such as, "I'm curious about this part . . . please tell me more."

We try not to make assumptions about artwork, but what if a child *wants* you to guess what they have made? This is tricky territory! If you guess right the first time, it could be validating, but chances are you will get it wrong. This could be insulting, especially if it takes several attempts before you get it right. What have you implied about the accuracy of the work? If in your best judgment it is best to decline, there is a way out: "Sorry, I'm not very good at guessing games, but I'm curious to know all about your painting!"

A child's artwork has its own reasoning. It may not be necessary for us to understand it at all. Creating it served a purpose. It is reason enough. But if a child chooses to talk about it, you may learn that there is far more to it than meets the eye. A simple purple circle can be a drawing of a curled-up sleeping cat. Or, seemingly random scribbles may actually be an intricate map of playground complete with swings, slides, seesaws, and spinners!

At first glance, the child shown in Figure 6.2 is holding a playful scrawling design. It would be easy to miss what Ella had intended. After listening to her description, however, it soon became clear that this was actually an intricate drawing of the art room. She had even written "Art Studio" on it in scattered letters! Her drawing of the table and chairs has a dynamic energy that captured the spirit of the room on that busy day!

As the famous art educator Robert Henri once observed, "All real works of art look as though they were done in joy. . . . Reveal the spirit. . . . Reality does not exist in material things. Rather paint the flying spirit of the bird than its feathers" (Henri 2007, 262–263).

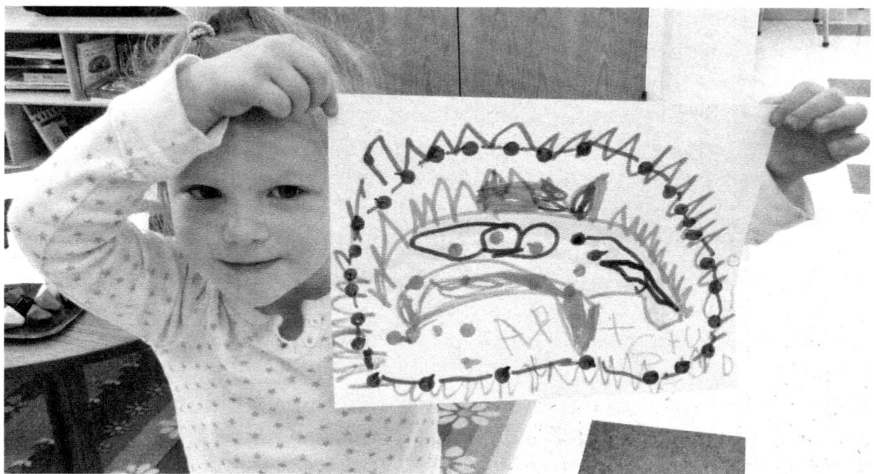

Figure 6.2   Artwork by Ella.

Creative young children don't use typical methods for conveying ideas, so it is a mistake to "correct" a unique visual vocabulary. Often, sizes, colors, and shapes won't be "accurate" according adult standards. Next to a purple lopsided house, a flower can sprout up higher than the rooftop. A pet pink polka dot turtle can float in midair. A smiling sun shines on even as rainclouds gather and drops drench the red grass where lollipops and candy canes will start to grow.

The process of making art has a magical quality for a young child. Ideas seem to flow ecstatically from an inner source without regard for logic. This artful play is important work, and it is also a delightful form of imaginative storytelling. If you are able to listen attentively while a child draws, you might overhear the dialogue of the players as they emerge from the page as if it were a stage.

WHY PRAISE HAS AN "INVERSE POWER"

Children's artwork can be full of wonders, but experts in child development warn us to avoid excessive praise; "This is the best painting I have ever seen!" is frankly unbelievable. Adults quickly lose credibility when they make ridiculous statements that are overly complimentary.

On the other hand, if frequent praise is somehow believed by the child, it can create a dependency on approval. Children may grow to need a high level of praise to feel valuable and validated in their work. "Excessive praise also distorts children's motivation; they begin doing things merely to hear the praise, losing sight of intrinsic enjoyment." This is termed *the inverse power of praise* (Bronson and Merryman 2009, 20–21).

We make the assumption that things work the same for children as they do for adults. The *Fallacy of Similar Effect* explains why we get it wrong when praising children. "In a variety of studies, praise has been shown to be effective on adults in workplaces. Grownups like being praised. While praise can undermine a child's intrinsic motivation, it doesn't have this effect on adults. It has the opposite effect: being praised by managers *increases* an adult's intrinsic motivation. . . . It's because we like praise so much that we intuited lavishing it upon kids would be beneficial" (237–238).

If we walk by, glancing and overpraising artwork, we diminish our credibility. Easy praise is quickly detected as unauthentic. At best it will be meaningless. At worst it can become an extrinsic reward that must be kept up—or else. If the reward is removed, so too goes the motivation of the person being praised. Relying on extrinsic motivation based on praise from outside sources can eventually cause a child to direct almost all efforts toward pleasing others. This may be satisfying for a while, but what happens when the praise is no longer there? Then the source of motivation can also disappear. What then will be the point of making an effort if high praise is no longer the reward?

Is all praise harmful for children? No. But praise that focuses only on product, rather than process, is to be avoided. Why is this so? Value judgments about the quality of art are *opinions* that say much more about the person making the judgment than about anything else. Even art experts disagree about what is fine art and what is not, and these opinions change over time. Value judgments both negative and positive can be problematic for young children.

Exclusively praising products also sets up the expectation that repeating this same work will lead to more praise. Rather than be motivated from within to try new ideas, children may tend to duplicate what has earned consistent approval and become reluctant to make other choices that might not be so successful. This narrows the flow of ideas to only the safe ones that have been tried and proven true. Supporting the effort and the process will free children to learn through discovery and expand their capabilities, rather than endlessly retracing ideas that won approval in the past.

Singling out one person for excessive praise is especially harmful in group settings. Everyone is listening, and this sends quite a different message to every other group member. Conversely, throwing a blanket of praise over an entire group is also not recommended, because it will obscure what is actually happening. Saying "Everyone is doing great!" denies that there are those with needs or insecurities in the room. Or, saying "You are all doing *beautiful* artwork!" denies that art making can have objectives other than beauty. When tempted to lavish praise on an entire group, beware that you are not really just praising yourself for running a group well. Any leader who is not following the diverse individual responses in the group is *not* being a facilitator of creativity.

> If you want to lead the people, you must learn how to follow them.
>
> —Lao Tzu, *Tao Te Ching,*
> Chapter 66

MINDSET AND THE POWER OF OUR BELIEFS

World-renowned researcher and psychologist Carol Dweck in her influential book *Mindset* has further cautions about the possible negative consequences of praise with children. She advised, "We should keep away from a certain *kind* of praise—praise that judges their intelligence or talent." She added, "We can praise them as much as we want for the growth-oriented process—what they accomplished through practice, study, persistence, and good strategies. And we can ask them about their work in a way that admires and appreciates their efforts and choices" (Dweck 2006, 172).

As an expert on the psychology of success, Dweck's research explores the impact of our beliefs on how we lead our lives. The belief that abilities such as intelligence or creativity are set and fixed and limited to an unchangeable quantity results in a *fixed mindset*. On the other hand, a *growth mindset*, Dweck explains, "is based on the belief that your basic qualities are things you can cultivate through your efforts" (7).

Many people believe that artistic (and creative) abilities are "carved in stone"—one either has them or not. They contend that these capacities are passed down through our genetic legacy, resulting in some being born "gifted." Others, who presumably lost this genetic lottery, will never have a chance to develop these artistic and creative qualities. An all-too-common question asked of creative people is this: "Who in your family gave your artistic abilities to you?" A surprising answer might be this: "I did. I made the decision to develop my artistic abilities."

Those with a fixed mindset tend to turn away from challenges or give up too soon. They protest, "I'm not really good at that anyway, so why should I try?" Fear of failure discourages taking chances. This thinking restricts what children believe about their learning potential. If they are told they have a scientific mind but also that they are not creative, how limiting would this be to their future as problem solver, innovator, inventor, or research scientist? Children can become reluctant to take on challenges that defy the boundaries that adult expectations set for them. When they avoid risking mistakes that might disappoint others, children give up before they begin.

A growth mindset, however, can lead to a passion and exuberance for learning and an ability to persist through challenges even when things are not going well. Because mindsets are based on beliefs, it is possible to make the choice to move from a fixed mindset toward a growth mindset. Doing so will enable us to become more courageous, more open to change, and less judgmental. This also means we will be able to encourage others to continue to develop in this way.

ENCOURAGING A GROWTH MINDSET

Being mindful in our interactions with children means analyzing whether we are encouraging a fixed or growth mindset. Comments intending to be praising and supportive can have underlying messages that are undermining and judgmental, leading to the development of fixed mindset thinking in children.

To support the development of a growth mindset, keep the emphasis on the art process. Encourage trying new experiences, experimentation, and coming up with strategies to overcome obstacles along the way. If mistakes are made, they can be a valuable resource for learning. How did the child manage to persist beyond these times of frustration? Instead of giving up, how was progress made? What new direction was taken? Through these experiences, children learn to persevere through difficulties, come up with strategies, and gain resilience. They can learn how to find the courage to move forward through challenges. This is *genuine* growth that generalizes into other experiences.

What then can a facilitator do when a child becomes "stuck" in the process and on the verge of giving up? Imagine, for instance, a child has been attempting to blend a light color and suddenly he cries out, "I can't do this!"

A facilitator can respond, "Let's see, you're trying to blend a light-blue color, but you haven't made it *yet* . . . OK, you started with mostly dark blue and then began to add white . . . Can you think of another way? . . . Oh, that's an idea . . . So, by starting with mostly white paint and blending a little blue, how is the color now? . . . Yes! Your strategy worked!" The use of the word *yet* is advocated by Carol Dweck to encourage a growth mindset. It conveys the reassurance that although it has not happened *yet*, it will happen.

It would have been counterproductive, of course, to blend the color for the child. Or even dictate the recipe of proportions for him to follow. He needed to discover—with a bit of guidance and just a little encouragement—how to find the way on his own. Notice, he never asked, "Do it for me." Children rarely do. The exception is the child who has been trained to make this request by adults who have over-assisted in the past. A child who has been taught helplessness will require considerably more encouragement to work toward independence. Many may decide to give up before they begin. They grow up saying, "I'm not creative."

When Sophie Thinks She Can't is a children's book by Molly Bang that was directly inspired by mindset research. There are also many wonderful children's books to inspire learning from mistakes. Among them are *The Beautiful Oops!* by Barney Saltzberg, *The Dot* by Peter H. Reynolds, and *It's Okay to Make Mistakes* by Todd Parr.

When we acknowledge the time spent during art making, we are valuing focused attention and persistence. When we commend experimentation, we are valuing curiosity, divergent thinking, learning from mistakes, and the use of alternative strategies. When we admire the choices made, we are valuing independent decision-making skills and self-reliance. The artwork is the by-product of this effort. Of course, not all art processes are intense and full of effort. Spontaneous and playful experiences can be instantly gratifying and a joy for anyone, but art is often work. It is art*work*, and although it may still be immensely pleasurable, it requires concentration, determination, and persistence to work through the process to completion.

Thoughtful admiration of effort will then be useful and well received. This places the emphasis where it belongs, on the child and on the process. When a child is intrinsically motivated, initiative comes from within. So the main objective of effective praise is to enable children to continuously access and develop their own authentic resources and autonomous capabilities.

When children are no longer dependent upon the praise of others as the main source of motivation, they can become self-starters. These individuals will be the *initiators* rather than the *imitators* of ideas. When freed from the requirement to seek approval and always please others, they will be more apt to endure criticism, make courageous choices, and persist against the odds despite setbacks. This is a creative mind, empowered to make a difference.

OVERCOMING IMPEDIMENTS TO CREATIVITY

When we decide to be creative, we can challenge our perceived limitations. We can break through obstructive barriers and envision alternative routes. We can see options, possibilities, make connections, and have fascinating encounters with the unexpected. From this we will gain the courage to take the risk to face future challenges. Or we can decide to stay safe.

Young children usually do not need much encouragement be creative. They do not see it as risky. Art making usually comes naturally. They splash like ducklings into the water. It is a delight to see! Without a moment's hesitation, young children leap into new art experiences and glide away to eagerly explore on their own.

Older children, teens, and adults often encounter an invisible barrier. It may last for moments or it may be there for a lifetime. Creative blocks are made of fear and doubt. This is their message: "Everything I do always comes out wrong. I envy people who make it look so easy. I have no talent. I didn't inherit the creative gene. Teachers told me that I was no good at art. I'm just not a creative person. I have no ideas."

We cannot deny these fears exist. The only way to get past creative blocks is to go through them. Without fear, there is no need for courage. If it takes courage to create, then self-doubt holds us back and risk-taking moves us forward.

A "creative resource" can flow through an inner landscape like a river. It can be wide, placid, and mirror reflective. Then with one turn around a bend, it becomes rocky, churning, and treacherous. A truly creative course leads away from the familiar toward the unexpected and ventures far into the unknown. There will be depths with an inky darkness below the shimmering surface. These journeys of imagination can lead into unexplored realms and onward to a luminous sea of possibilities.

Everyone's inner landscape is unique. It takes courage to navigate these waters alone. There can be collaborative adventures, but most often it is a solitary journey. There are guides, but they only take us so far. The direction of creativity is by its very nature unpredictable. We can only discover where it will take us when we are well along the way. Just as rivers can shape the surrounding landscape over time, the flow of creativity can be central to our self-definition. It is what we make of ourselves and who we become.

In order to become facilitators, we need to be aware of what can hinder the creative process and learn from those who encounter and overcome blocks to creativity. One of the major impediments is perfectionism. Author Julia Cameron describes how anguishing the pursuit of perfection can be: "Perfectionism is a blocking device." It is a "debilitating loop" that drives us crazy. Cameron adds, "When we erase until the paper tears, or see our children doing this, we must halt the obsession. Perfectionism is not a quest for the

True perfection seems imperfect,
yet it is perfectly itself. . .
True wisdom seems foolish.
True art seems artless.

—Lao Tzu, *Tao Te Ching*,
Chapter 45

best—it is the pursuit of the worst in ourselves, the part that tells us we will never be good enough. Perfection is egotism parading as virtue. Do not be fooled. We are good enough. And our children are good enough, as well" (Cameron and Lively 2013, 196).

ASSISTING THE PROCESS

Even when it is under the guise of pleasure, artwork is still work. It can be fraught with frustrations and difficulties that may seem insurmountable. "Our task, regarding creativity," according to educator Loris Malaguzzi, "is to help children climb their own mountains, as high as possible. No one can do more" (Malaguzzi 1993, 71).

It is the challenge of the climb that brings the thrill of accomplishment. We cannot carry our children; they must climb for themselves.

There will be times, however, when children feel stranded in the art process. Encouraging effort and persistence will not be enough. They need another level of support. Here is a description of what can happen: a child has been drawing and erasing, doing and undoing for a while, and muttering, "I just can't do this . . . Oh no! . . . What am I doing? This is all wrong . . . I can't draw!"

Facilitators understand that being truly helpful means providing the least intrusive method of assistance. One can begin simply by asking, "What is it you were trying to do?"

It is not unusual for a child to become frustrated when trying to draw images from memory, such as a dolphin. If so, then ask if a photograph would be helpful. In a library, it is easy enough to find resources in books.

A photo image may be all that is necessary for some children to find their own way. If not, please remember to provide just enough structure (what educators call "scaffolding") to enable children to do the work for themselves. Absolutely never draw on any child's artwork. In fact, it is best not to draw at all. This way, the child is not obliged to copy your work. Instead, enable the child to think it through, by saying something like this: "What is the basic shape of a dolphin's body? . . . Oh, they are long and curved . . . Where would you begin to make a line like that on your paper?"

Observe and respect that once the child is working independently, it is time to quietly step away.

The open-ended process is not about being right or wrong, good or bad. If we say products are "perfect!" or "outstanding!" we are voicing strong value judgments. Even in the affirmative, there is an underlying message being sent that misdirects our intentions. Creativity is not about being compliant with following our instructions. These experiences are not about being perfect. It is not about competition with others to win our approval. It is about the creative *process* teaching the child, not *us* teaching the child.

It is true that both unrealistically high and exceedingly low expectations can be damaging. Ultimately, both result in thoughts like these: "What's the use of trying? I'll never measure up, anyway." This self-sabotage destroys creative initiative. Regardless of how high the aptitude may be, a defeatist attitude will surely crush potential. Everyone knows people who have given up. They no longer play the piano or create paintings because they could not make it in the professional world. They may even speak about these losses with great regret, yet they have chosen to leave it all behind. Fear often blocks the way. Fear of being second-rate, fear of being negatively compared to others, fear of being judged.

How does anyone get past this? To borrow an expression taken from an aptly named song titled "Come from the Heart": "You've got to dance like nobody's watchin'." Of course, we can dance, play the piano, and paint much more freely when no one *critically judgmental* and negative is watching. So how do we create such a nonjudgmental place?

We design an environment where it is safe to experiment and go beyond the fear of mistakes; a place to search without really knowing what will be found, where the process becomes the teacher; a place to freely explore creative possibilities.

Once in this environment, how do we enable others to get past their own *inner* obstacles? We all encounter these internal barriers of fear. Somewhere along the way we learned how to move forward. We just need to remember *how* in order to enable others to do the same. First, we find a way to get past the internal censor, the critic who forever judges "good" and "bad" art. This critic has existed forever. It is back there among our early memories. The critic could have been an older brother who laughed at our "stupid" drawings. The critic could have been a teacher who drew on our art to "make it better" before it qualified for the art show. The critic could be a parent who decided we were just not "gifted" in art. Criticism that once was outside us inevitably crept inside to become an obstacle, a creative block.

Accomplished artists struggle every day with the internal critic. Due to their extensive experience, they have some of the best advice on how to help others get past creative blocks. Many artists wisely advise to work small. Authors put it this way: start writing a page, not a book. Daily jotting in a notebook is invariably recommended. But then how does the artist face the notorious blank canvas? Again, the advice often is to work small; draw daily in sketchbooks and paint quickly on small canvases.

The small format frees the ability to experiment while decreasing fear of failure. There is no longer a concern about making a major work of art or masterpiece. Artists advise that reducing the size of the "blank canvas" or other surface can make the art process seem less intimidating. This is especially true for adults, teens, and older children who are reluctant to experiment with art materials on larger surfaces. Offering six-by-six-inch papers in generous

> Confront the difficult
> while it is still easy;
> accomplish the great task
> by a series of small acts.
>
> —Lao Tzu, *Tao Te Ching*,
> Chapter 63

quantities can open up possibilities, but the choice to size up to larger paper should always be honored as an option. (It must be noted, however, that the youngest of children need large-size paper to encourage scribbling freely with expanded movements.)

Chuck Close is an artist not known for small canvases. He is world-renowned for astonishingly realistic portraits of faces that can measure 10 feet tall. These paintings, however, are actually a compilation of smaller areas painted within a grid that together form the faces. What makes his artwork all the more astounding is that Chuck Close is paralyzed, and he paints with a brush strapped to his arm. Quoted in Danielle Krysa's *Creative Block*, Chuck Close has something to say to all of us about the art process, overcoming creative blocks, and motivation: "I work. This is the only way for me. I work through, or around, a 'block.' . . . All the best ideas come out of the process; they come out of the work itself. Things occur to you" (Krysa 2014, 125).

So it is the *process* that inspires. This means a facilitator enables process of art itself to be the inspiration. When a work of art is done this way, artwork will not feel like work at all.

TRUSTING THE PROCESS

Designing art experiences to be open-ended means trusting that others are capable of finding their own way. A facilitator of creativity gives just enough guidance to enable each group participant to take a solitary journey, not knowing where it will lead but knowing that this is the way to develop creative resources and confidence.

It is an act of trust to take solitary journey of discovery. It is safer to follow the pack than to find one's own way. When there are no directions, it is not easy to envision all the possibilities and find the courage to choose among them. Because there is no set destination, there will be no clear standard to measure how much has been accomplished or how far there is yet to go. The open-ended process can be the means to an end. More likely, it is a means to a beginning. It is a start. The inquiry is opened without providing any of the answers.

Where does it go from there? Curiosity is a powerful motivator in art, especially for young children. Most of us can learn from children how to allow curiosity to overcome all the nagging anxieties that uncertainty thrusts in the way. Having the courage to follow our own inquisitiveness will lead rapidly away from the familiar and into the great unknown. No one else around us in the group is going the same way. Every decision we make leads to another. What urges us on is not what others are pursuing. The more that individual choices are being made, the greater our directions will differ from one another. Each participant in an open art group will not be competing with others but, instead, exploring a unique set of challenges and self-determined solutions.

> It overcomes without competing,
> answers without speaking a word,
> arrives without being summoned,
> accomplishes without a plan.
>
> —Lao Tzu, *Tao Te Ching*, Chapter 73

If the process goes awry for a while—especially when it becomes quite challenging—this can be the most effective way to learn. Now staying with the process can result in the expansion of creative resources, improved abilities to persevere, and the development of resilience in the face of adversity. This is the *work* of artwork, and it takes practice and patience. But with many such encounters, the result will be in a sense of mastery and creative confidence. This is why a creativity facilitator does not rush to the rescue by offering more support than is necessary. It would impede, rather than encourage, growth through the creative process.

7

Collaborative Murals

CONSTRUCTING OUR TOWN

Our Town was inspired by a mural created at the Eric Carle Museum of Picture Book Art entitled *Carleville* posted on the Web site by Diana MacKenzie in 2014.

Our Town was the first collaborative mural created in Open Art Studio and represents a welcoming neighborhood inclusive of everyone. The intent was to bring multigenerational participants together by working toward a common goal.

The black cardstock "roads" were constructed on the wall by library staff. On a nearby art table, an array of geometric cardstock shapes were offered, along with glue, scissors, and markers. Over a series of sessions, the neighborhood was creatively constructed and "built up" with a wide array of homes and structures. No two houses were the same. Each had their own distinctive style and detail. Elaborate modern "dream home" structures stood alongside charming little cottages. One small house had a lift-the-flap window that revealed a person peering out from inside. A few of the houses had an "X-ray" view of furniture or activities going on within the rooms. Some of the houses had humanlike features, and one house even sprouted arms and legs!

Our Town remained on the library wall for years. During that time, many children would stand before the mural and fondly "revisit" the home they had left there.

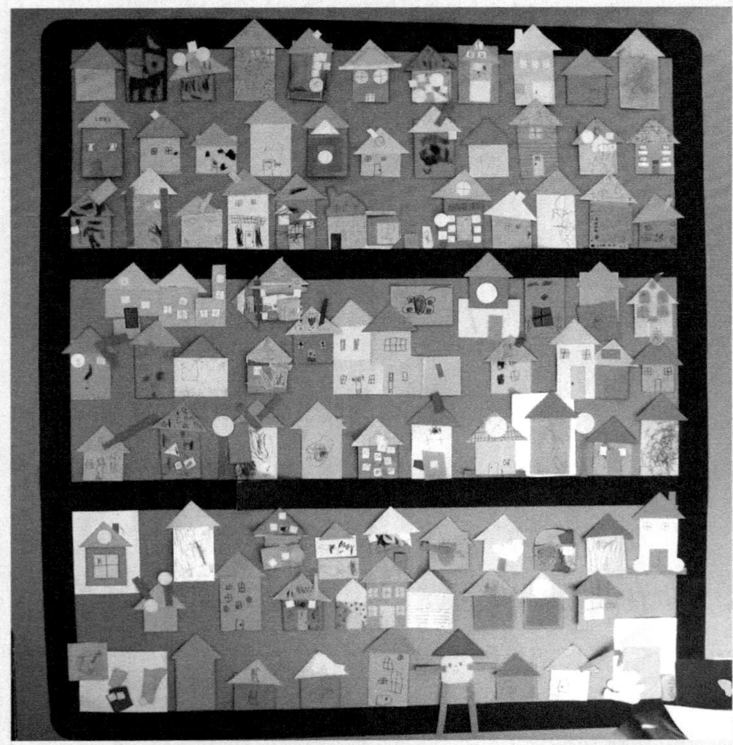

Figure 7.1   *Our Town*. Photograph courtesy of the Avon Free Public Library.

OUR TOWN

Multicolor cardstock

Black cardstock

Fine and broad-tip markers

Glue sticks

Scissors

Removable mounting putty

Preparation: Protect the table with brown craft paper.

Use black cardstock to define a road on the wall using removable mounting putty.

Cut the multicolor cardstock into a variety of sizes of geometric shapes.

Table Setup: Place the geometric cardstock down the center of a long table, with glue sticks and markers nearby.

Provide scissors on request.

Guidelines: Everyone will make a house. Together, it will be our town.

Variations: Plan a city of the future.

Design an amusement park.

Establish a settlement on another planet.

Discover an ancient magical realm.

What else?

CREATING THE FISH IN THE SEA

The Fish in the Sea mural was inspired by the books *Only One You* and *You Be You*, written and illustrated by Linda Kranz. The author's words encourage individuality and embolden exploration, while her illustrations of brightly painted rockfish are charmingly expressive of these ideas.

The Fish in the Sea mural was created over a summer, beginning as a special art experience during the annual event Art Day in May at the library. On the day the mural began, dozens of people stopped by to contribute fish to the window mural. Babies made little scribbles on their fish, while older siblings wrote their name, carefully practicing and pronouncing each letter. Many children made striped or dotted fish. A few drew themselves riding on fish! Some other children dutifully changed the surface of the fish from one color to an entirely different color. A few older children, teens, and adults drew intricate scales and fins with kaleidoscopic detail. There were kissing fish, rainbow fish, and fish with tiny eggs inside. One tropical fish wore sunglasses and a bathing suit! The amazing diversity of these fish proved that cutouts do not have to be cliché crafts. When cutouts are rendered with such an array of fanciful, original, and imaginative ideas, they will go beyond craft and into the realm of art.

It must be admitted that quite a few fish "got away." This is the way of collaboration—not everyone collaborates! Sometimes, young children start out with the intention of giving the fish away and then change their minds. So, it was with a smile and a wave that we sent these creations home with their creators. But just before they left, we asked to take a photo of the artwork. This was invariably accepted as a deal. One kept the fish but left behind the image. We asked if we could use the photo of the fish for the mural. This is invariably taken as a compliment and satisfied everyone.

If there was time, it was requested that another fish be made for the mural. This offer was usually accepted, but it was not surprising when the other fish went home, too! This is especially true with littlest ones, who may not comprehend why they should ever let go of their artwork. It must always be taken into consideration that it is their property, after all. If there was even the slightest hesitation, it was made clear that it was their choice whether to keep or give it away. Only when it is freely chosen to give art to the mural, should it be accepted. Always these offerings were accepted with gratitude.

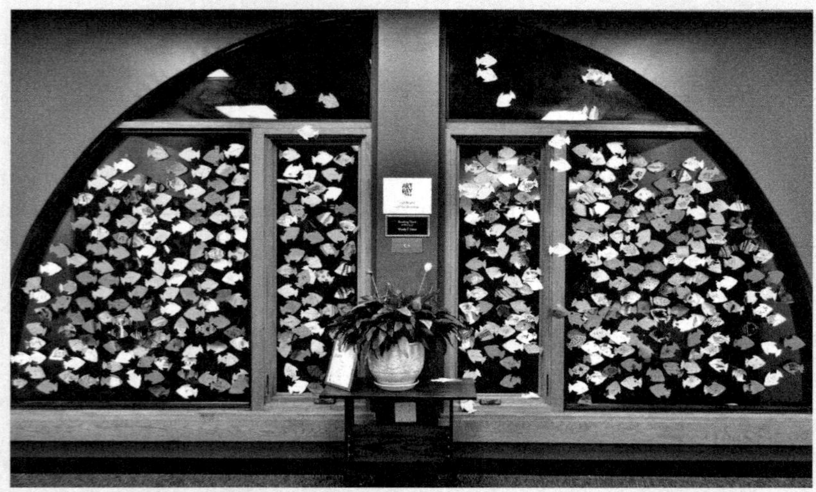

Figure 7.2   Fish in the Sea. Photograph courtesy of the Avon Free Public Library.

FISH IN THE SEA

Multicolor cardstock
Fine- and broad-tip markers
Paint markers
Tape

Preparation: Cut fish shapes from a variety of colored cardstock.
Prepare a sign: Everyone create a fish!
Table Setup: Set up a table near a window.
Provide markers and tape.
With groups of children over five, teens, and adults, provide paint markers.
Guidelines: Everyone will make a fish. Each one will be unique.
They will be taped to the window, and together they will swim in the sea!

Variations: Try this idea with other shapes: Flowers, birds, or butterflies.

Combine these ideas to create a world with fish below and flowers and butterflies above.

Create a sky mural or mobile with butterfly or bird shapes.

Make a window mural of a tree with leaf shapes.

What else?

CONSTRUCTING CITY COLLAGE

This collage was inspired by the art studio at the Eric Carle Museum of Picture Book Art as seen in a blog post by Meg Nicoll on January 30, 2017. Their original Collaborative Window Collage was based on the ridgeline of the Holyoke Range near the museum and was first outlined with black masking tape before the tissue was applied by visitors to the art studio.

City Collage was inspired by the Hartford skyline, featuring the shapes of prominent buildings outlined by staff with blue masking tape. Completed in a single day, City Collage was a collaborative project during Art Day in May at the library. Over a period of hours, many people became involved in the project. Some stayed for a short while; others remained to complete major portions of the mural. Adults had to stretch to reach the upper areas, and children kneeled down to reach the lower sections. Fragments of torn tissue were applied to the glass using foam brushes dipped in liquid laundry starch as adhesive. Every now and then someone would step back and say, "Wow!"

The mural banished the dull view of a parking lot below. Instead, there was a luminous cohesion of hues that flung refracted color deep into the room. At times, the mural cast surprisingly strong structural shadows of the city across the carpeted floor. It was both bold and fragile.

Window collages such as this are intended to be temporary works of art. The stability and adhesion will be impacted by both temperature and humidity. It is reasonable to expect that a similar collage can remain about a month or so on a window. It may stay longer if skillfully applied and periodically maintained by reattaching areas that become unfastened. The edges of the collage will gradually separate from the window, and eventually the entire work can be taken down. Some parts will peel away with little effort. Other areas can be loosened by first saturating sections with soapy water or a glass cleaner and waiting for it to penetrate. A soft scrub brush or a plastic scraper with rounded edges will assist in removal without scratching the glass.

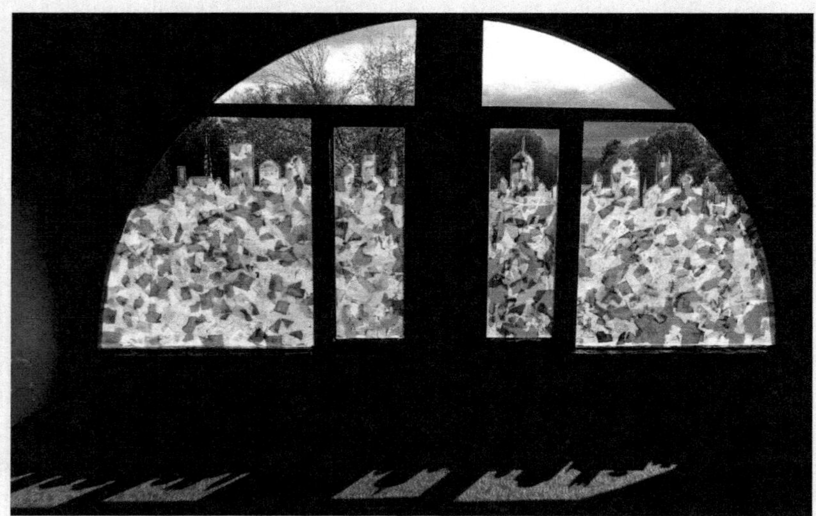

Figure 7.3   City Collage. Photograph courtesy of the Avon Free Public Library.

CITY COLLAGE

A large window (with a view that can be obstructed)

Blue or black painter's tape (use ½ inch or 1 inch width)

Torn tissue paper (yellow, pink, blue, green)

Liquid laundry starch

1-inch foam brushes with wooden handles

Plastic cups

Preparation: Use painter's tape to outline a city skyline on a window.

Select 4 to 5 coordinating tissue colors to tear and place into bins (or participants later tear tissue colors of their choice).

Shake to mix liquid starch and pour into small plastic containers.

Place a foam brush in each container.

Protect lower parts of the windowsill from drips with tape and plastic wrap.

Table Setup: On a small nearby table, set up a workstation with a tissue bins.

Pour liquid starch in cups with foam brushes.

Display a sign explaining the art process (optional).

Guidelines: Explain that this is a collaborative mural of a city.

It will be temporary.

Torn tissue will be applied to the glass using the liquid starch.

Saturate a small area of glass with the liquid and place a piece of tissue on top.

Wet the tissue again while smoothing with the foam brush.

Encourage experimentation with overlapping and layering tissue.

Variations: Tissue can be torn or precut.

Try contrasting warm and cool colors on separate sections of a mural.

Variations can be inspired by different representational themes and landscapes.

A window collage may also be a structured design or freeform abstraction.

THOUGHTS ON THE TREE OF DIVERSITY: HANDS THROUGH TIME

The silhouettes, prints, stencils, and outlines of human hands have been found in prehistoric cave art around the world. Discovered in diverse regions such as France, Argentina, Borneo, and Australia, there is an astonishing frequency and consistency in these findings. They have a stunning resemblance to our own hands, and yet these symbols mark the *beginning* of recorded human history. On the walls of Chauvet Cave in southern France, the image of a hand identifiable by a crooked little finger may merge the artist's art and signature.

Now we understand this enduring connection. When children draw around their own small hands, they are outlining the edges of who they are. Children will choose to make handprints and silhouettes using any material available to them. Whether outlined with markers, printed with paint, or pressed into clay, they delight in making their mark and leaving impressions of themselves. This innocent urge may still be in all of us somewhere. Creating a unique handprint is an ancient signature that profoundly defines each one of us.

Handprints can be the inspiration for numerous art experiences working with all ages. The Tree of Diversity is a mural with handprints placed on a tree as if they were "leaves." Along with the children, many adults also participated. So did members of the library staff. The author's handprint is among them. Together we became an array of colors moving across the spectrum, adorning the same tree. It is harmony in diversity.

THE TREE OF LIFE

Symbolic images of the tree of life have been created throughout the history of the world. Inspired by Klimt's swirling *Tree of Life*, the library art studio has a blank blue wall ideal for a majestic mural like this. Many contemporary collaborative murals feature hands as leaves. Our own mural was inspired by the spectrum of color on the Family Tree found on the blog at the J.W. Killam School in Massachusetts, posted by teacher Amy Hussey, who has generously shared it with others. Now, we share it with you.

This eloquent expression of diversity will be even more effective if it can continue to be recreated in schools, libraries, and other public buildings. An idea such as this can gain intensity and resonate with new meaning when taken into other contexts. This paper mural will exist only for a limited time. But if the idea is not confined to a single place, it can continue to have an ever widening influence. Such ideas are meant to be shared . . . and so we pass them on and invite others to do the same.

The Tree of Diversity was created over a period of months by just about everyone who came into the art studio during that period. It was an adjunct to the main programming for that session and was just one of many art experiences available during Open Art Studio. Each participant chose a color from the cardstock and worked with either regular markers or paint markers. Adults with young children traced their hands and sometimes assisted in cutting out the shape, but the children placed their own marks and ideas on the surfaces. One child drew a tiny fairy in her hand. Older children, teens, and adults devoted considerable time to making elaborate designs, images, or writing messages of hope on their hand shape before it was placed as a leaf on the Tree of Diversity.

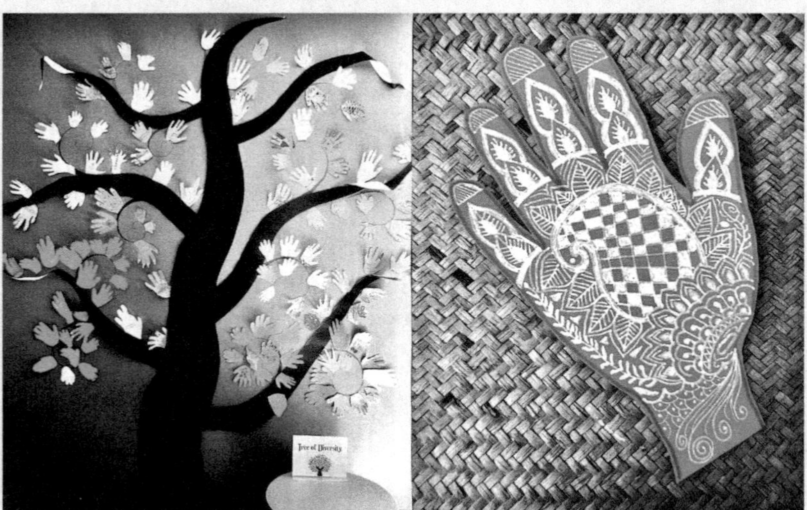

Figure 7.4   The Tree of Diversity. Photograph courtesy of the Avon Free Public Library. Enlarged detail of Hand/Leaf by Nupur Gupta.

Tree of Diversity

Black-and-white dual-sided paper roll, 48" × 12' (or brown butcher block
    paper roll)

Cardstock (bright colors—assorted rainbow colors)

Fine- and broad-tip markers

Water-based paint markers

Preparation: Use the paper roll to cut a tree trunk.

Place on a wall using removable mounting putty.

Cut and place lower branches.

Work up to smaller branches while balancing side to side.

Twist branch ends, if desired.

Cut up various colors of cardstock for "leaves."

Cut 9" × 12" cardstock in half to make 9" × 6" pieces for adult hands.

Cut again to make 4½" × 6" pieces for child hands.

Table Setup: Place cut cardstock on a long table by arranging the color
    spectrum: red, orange, yellow, green, blue, indigo, and violet.

Set markers on the table.

Guidelines: Explain that everyone can choose to take part in a collaborative
    mural by making a hand design that will be placed as a leaf on the tree (or
    make two leaves and take one home).

Encourage participants to use the markers to make each hand a personal
    expression.

CREATING OCEAN, LAND, SKY, AND SPACE

The collaborative mural of Ocean, Land, Sky, and Space was created by
a group of children age five through eight in the Creative Art program.
Over the summer, they met once a week for an hour. The plan was to make
a very large mural by piecing it together one section at a time. Each long
section began flat on a table. Every child had access to glue sticks, scissors,
markers, and an array of cardstock colors. Everyone came up with ideas of
their own that fit the broad theme of the week, such as "sky."

Most of the children concentrated on their own separate pieces. Some
specialized in 3-D objects, such as the folded paper airplanes, for the
mural. At times, the children delegated duties: one was chosen to draw
directly on the mural, while others created individual pieces. A few older
children became "helpers" with cutting or pasting for the younger ones. If
something was agreeable to all, then this was how it was done, at least for
a while. By the end of each session, all the decisions were made as to where
the pieces would be glued onto the larger panel. After some spirited debate
and negotiations, locations were found that were acceptable to all.

As to be expected, some children wanted to keep the piece that they created and bring it home. So they were encouraged to make a second piece to contribute to the mural. Also, the children persuaded each other to let go of things for the sake of the mural. Flattery went a long way! "Your alien spaceship is great. You can launch it from my planet!"

Playfulness was one of the most exciting aspects of mural making. Once children cut out their drawings, the little creatures that were liberated became more "real." Children played with them imaginatively as if they were toys. An octopus magically swam through the air; a trumpeting elephant stomped cheerily; and the birds sang as they flew, before quietly consenting to being glued to the mural.

The spirit of play continued over the weeks as the mural progressed in layers up the wall, starting with the ocean and ending with the final panel of "space." When the upper section was finally placed, it was fixed to a sloping ceiling so that the space section curved overhead! The children were awed by what they had accomplished.

Over the months that the mural was displayed, those who participated in making it brought friends and family over to the wall to admire it. Many photos were taken by parents of children, who proudly pointed to their contribution on the mural. The impact was quite impressive, and the massive mural became a marvelous way to announce the existence of the art program to those who previously had been unaware of it. People walking by the mural would stop and linger there for a while, smiling with amazement.

OCEAN, LAND, SKY, AND SPACE

4 Paper rolls 48" × 12' long: 2 blue shades, 1 green, and 1 black

Multicolor cardstock

Fine- and broad-tip markers

Glue sticks

Scissors

Book tape to mount to mural to wall (use a wall that will not be damaged by this strong adhesive)

Table Setup: Place unrolled long paper on a separate table.

Set up all other supplies on the main worktable.

Guidelines: This mural will take four sessions to complete.

First will be the lowest section of the ocean, followed by land, sky, and space.

Everyone will create their own separate pieces for the mural.

Each of these pieces will be glued to the long paper at the end of each session.

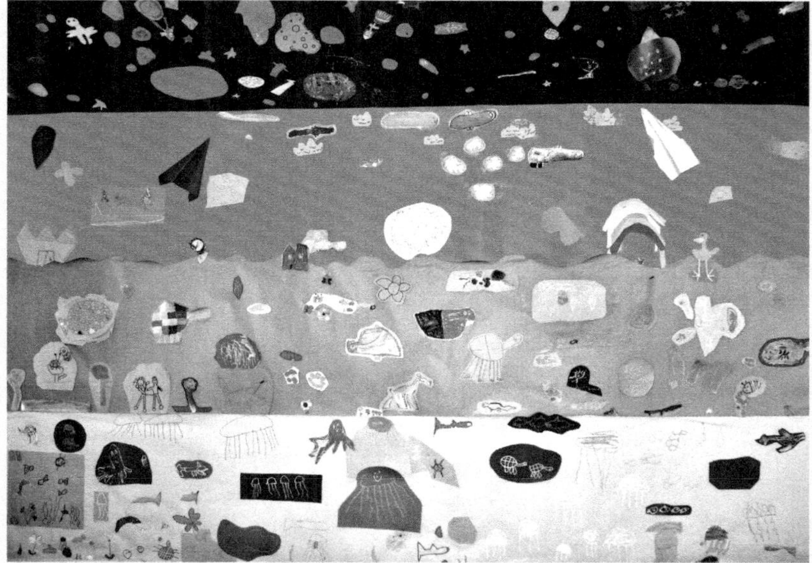

Figure 7.5   Ocean, Land, Sky, and Space. Photograph courtesy of the Avon Free Public Library.

When possible, participants will assist in applying the finished sections to the wall.

Variations: An exciting variation would be to create a collaborative *mobile* using ocean, sky, or space as a theme.

Movement will enhance the idea of being under sea, up the air, or out in space.

CREATING TOGETHER

Together on a Mural was created in a single summer day session with children in a Creative Art group entering grades one through three in the fall. The background paper had been pre-painted to dry beforehand. Eighteen children took part in making self-portraits using paint markers on cardstock. A teen volunteer assisted some of the younger children, who asked for help to cut out and to place the figures they had drawn for the mural.

The portraits now appear serene, but it was a boisterous group that created these images! Enthusiastic chatter and energy filled the room during the process. Everyone wanted to talk about what they were doing. One child decided to draw what he was wearing that day, and many others were inspired to do the same. Children delighted in describing themselves while adding stripes, T-shirt emblems, tutus, dress patterns, tied sneaker laces, and hair bows. Some older children helped the younger ones to cut out their figures. There was an enchanting "paper doll effect" once the images were set free, as the children playfully walked the drawings over and talked with one another.

Many children decided to make more than one self-portrait and proudly took the other home, although deciding which "self" should stay behind was not always an easy decision! Somehow all the work came together in the end. This mural reflects the diversity of the exuberant young artists who came together to make it and affirms the joyful spirit of creation.

Together on a Mural has continued to hang for years just inside the entrance to the Art Studio and has come to represent the essence of what can take place there.

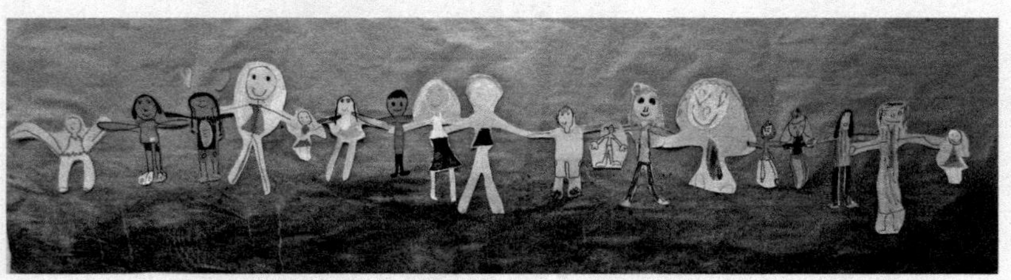

Figure 7.6 *Together on a Mural.* Photograph courtesy of the Avon Free Public Library.

TOGETHER ON A MURAL

Paper roll 36" × 6' long

Multicolor cardstock

Fine- and broad-tip markers

Paint markers

Glue sticks

Scissors

Adhesive to mount the mural to the wall: removable mounting putty

Table Setup: Place unrolled long paper on a separate table.

Set up all other supplies on the main worktable.

Offer a range of skin-toned papers placed down the center of the table.

Guidelines: Each child creates a self-portrait.

At the end of the session, each of these portraits will be applied to the mural.

If possible, participants will assist in applying the finished sections to the wall.

Variations: Various backgrounds can be created with the assistance of the
group:

These can be seasonal or locational (urban, rural, etc.).

At a playground (designed by the children) or at the zoo.

The self portraits can be extended to imaginary ideas: If I were an animal,
what kind would I be?

Collaborations such as these are first and foremost an experience. Most of the artwork described in this chapter no longer exists. It was known from the beginning that these massive murals were ephemeral and designed not to last. What endures happens during the process. It involves the art of listening and the art of compromise. People envision, interact, disagree, decide, laugh, inspire, and admire each other. It is both expressive art and the art of expression. Once again, the value goes beyond our systems of measurement. Indeed, the collective triumph is more than the sum of its parts.

8

Art with Multigenerational Groups

PAINTING IN A LIBRARY

No art material has quite the allure of paint. Of all art media, it is most classically associated with "being an artist." Yet the idea of painting can conjure doubts and initial resistance. It can be messy, difficult to control, and the outcome is often unpredictable, even for an expert. Yet this is exactly why it is such a valuable creative experience.

How could anyone attempt to offer painting sessions in a place such as a public library—the place most associated with rules, regulations, and meticulous systems of organization down to its decimal points? Here, above all, orderliness is valued, and all is well when everything is in its place.

How can creative art experiences thrive in this setting? It may not be easy, but it is simple. It requires adapting to the environment and working with the system, rather than against it. When this is done well, change will come in increments, slowly, over time. Remember that even the most positive of changes will have an element of stress for those involved.

Where do you begin? Start with the basics. How can painting with children conform to the requirements of a library setting or any other public building? How do we contain messiness? First, find tables that are sized for children, but also not too small for the adult caregivers.

It is advised that trays and no-spill paint cups be purchased. Our library learned from the advice of the art studio staff at the Eric Carle Museum of Picture Book Art. Invest in good-quality brushes, and use paint materials that are durable, such as large tempera cakes. If the budget allows, purchase a multilayered drying rack for wet paintings. All these initial investments will pay off well over the years to come.

Invest in quality. Buy large sheets (12" × 18") of good-quality watercolor paper in bulk and cut it down to save on expenses. Smaller (6" × 6") squares of paper are much less intimidating than large paper. The smaller size also encourages experimentation. Be generous by offering as many small sheets as needed to group participants.

Invest in large (2.25" × .75") nontoxic tempera paint blocks (also called cakes). A typical set of six disk-shaped paints in a tray will have black, and also the primary colors: blue, red, and yellow. Such sets also come with the secondary color block of green, which is supplementary, since green can easily be mixed from the primary colors blue and yellow. White is also included in the set of six, which can be useful for learning to create lighter opaque tints, such as pink from red.

These generously sized blocks of paint will last through many years of painting sessions. Each color can be purchased separately when there is a need to replenish just part of the set. These paints share some similarities with pan watercolors, but the large size of the tempera cakes makes them much more durable and long lasting. The dry pigment easily liquefies and intensifies when stroked with a wet brush.

When working with multigenerational groups, especially with young children, try offering a limited palette. Start with one at a time, beginning with black paint or blue paint. Why do this? Because it simplifies and centers the attention. The focus will be on coming to grips with brushes, practicing pigment intensity, and trying different ways to apply the paint. Young children are fascinated by this experimentation. Do they miss having all the colors? Apparently not. Older children, teens, and adults may wonder why it is limited this way, but they will be surprised to discover how expressive paint can be, even with only one color.

There are many books with art and illustrations that are mainly in black and white, such as *Kitten's First Full Moon* by Kevin Henkes. Objects such as china in the traditional Blue Willow pattern also convey the idea of a limited palette. Objects, books, or photos of art can be set to the side somewhere in the room to be discovered by curious observers, rather than to be shown as examples of how to do it "right."

The single paint choice method is an excellent way to introduce painting sessions with large groups in a public place. It is practical because of its simplicity. Group members can efficiently concentrate on the painting process uninterrupted because there is no need to constantly refresh the water. If the water cup darkens with color, it will not be a distracting problem and may actually aid the painting process by painting directly from the pigmented water. This will also be the case when painting with two colors; young children will be fascinated by the orange water that suddenly appears in their cup when they paint with red and yellow!

With each additional color added, offer more brushes, paper towels for wiping, and a way to change the water more frequently. Painting with the primaries—red, yellow, and blue—will require thoughtful planning on how to provide an easy source of clear water and a way for everyone to rinse brushes.

Never underestimate the power of quality paints. Skimping here is a common error. Avoid cheap pan watercolor sets that are quickly used up. They are no bargain. Buy quality paints in bulk (but avoid inexpensive off-brands). Liquid tempera paint can be purchased in gallons with dispenser tops. Start with basic black and white. Try painting with black liquid tempera on white paper—or white tempera on black paper—each has a strong dramatic contrast that will be especially compelling for young children. Invest in primary colors. Secondary colors are not necessary because they can be easily mixed. If budget allows, however, bright neon or florescent colors are especially exciting on both light and dark papers.

Quality brushes are equally important. A poor quality brush is the best way to convince someone that they are *not* an artist. No matter what they do, it will end in frustration. Terrible brushes are stocked in abundance in arts and crafts closets. Some may have once been adequate but were badly cleaned and stored over the years. Now bent over, hardened, and mangled, it is merciful to throw them away. But please don't replace them with something as bad or worse, just to save money.

Many paintbrushes sold in bulk or marketed for children are extremely inexpensive but still not worth the price. These brushes are easy to find, dropping their bristles just about everywhere they go. Open cheap water-color sets intended for children: there they will be. Everything about them is wrong: they are too small, too poorly made of cheap plastic, and the stiff black bristles splay every which way and then fall out. There is no point, literally, in working with them.

Good-quality brushes have a point, or an edge, and they are neither too large nor too small. Giant-size brushes with thick handles are wonderful for large expansive painting, especially at an easel or on a mural. But for smaller works, it is best to scale the size of the brush to the suit the size of the surface. Select brushes appropriate for the type of paint to be used and for the hands that will be using them. Round brushes with sizes 8 to 14 are recommended for most tasks, but keep a variety of sizes and types on hand. Quality brushes can be made of natural and synthetic materials. Good handles may be of wood or high-quality plastic. Quality brushes will not shed or fall apart easily. Never let brushes soak in water for long. With due diligence in cleaning and upright storage, quality brushes will endure the test of time.

Having a variety of brush sizes and types—round, angled, and flat—for each person in the group is ideal. Each brush will respond in a different way that will invite experimentation. Exploring the thick and thin edges of flat and chiseled brushes can be as rewarding as finding other brushes that render flowing undulating lines, or precise dots. The expressive possibilities of paint will be deepened and widened. If so, don't be surprised to hear someone say, "I never knew I could paint!"

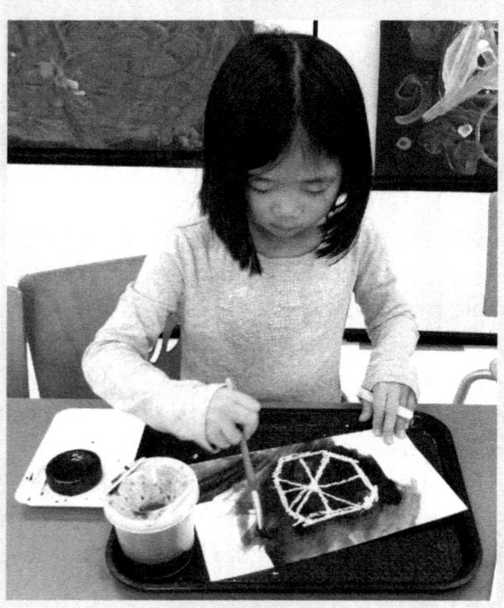

Figure 8.1 Sarah Chung creating an oil pastel resist painting.

TEMPERA BLOCK PAINTING WITH OIL PASTEL RESIST

White watercolor paper

Tempera blocks (cakes)

Paint trays, brushes, no-spill paint cups (clear with clear or white lids)

White oil pastels

Paper towels

Preparation: Cut the watercolor paper into 6" × 6" squares.

Put water to the fill line on no-spill cups, and place lids with an opening on each one.

Make a sign explaining the art process (optional): Create a resist painting by first drawing with oil pastel and then painting over it. The drawing will show through the paint!

Table Setup: Protect the table with a plastic tablecloth and brown craft paper.

On individual trays, place no-spill cups, watercolor paper, and a variety of brushes.

Place a single tempera block on each tray (black or blue recommended for high contrast).

(Use the flat lid of the cup as a container for the paint block).

Place oil pastels and folded paper towels near all trays.

Place a sign explaining resist painting on the table (optional).

Guidelines: Briefly say how resist paintings are made by drawing first with white oil pastel on the paper. It will not be easy to see, but when it is painted over with dark paint, the white oil pastel drawing will be revealed!

Encourage experimentation.

Variations

Later sessions: Try two color combinations, such as red/yellow or blue/yellow or red/blue. Paint with the three primary colors.

Paint on geometric shapes from watercolor paper or cutouts of leaves, butterflies, birds, etc.

The most effective resist contrast is achieved using light colors of oil pastel and applying a wash of dark paint on top.

Also try using dark oil pastels, and paint over with a light-color wash (such as yellow).

DRAWING WITH PAINT: WATER-BASED PAINT MARKERS

Paint markers blend the fluidity of paint together with the capacity to make a crisp line. When we use them, we are actually *drawing with paint.* Exciting to explore, the process can be mesmerizing and result in a product unlike anything else. It is understandable why such an art experience would appeal to all ages. But paint markers are best introduced when children have the fine motor control to reasonably manage them. It will be necessary to learn how to hold the marker at the angle that allows for a consistent flow. With too little pressure, the line of paint will appear scratchy, unpredictable, or seem to "dry up." With too much pressure, the paint will ooze and puddle. Usually, children around the age of five or six can learn how to control the paint marker enough to be very pleased with the results.

Paint markers can be expensive, so try to invest in just a few at first. Sets of silver and gold are a good first choice. The metallic colors have a shimmering quality that is fun and festive. Most paper colors have an interesting interplay with paint markers. While regular markers are lost on dark paper, it is just the opposite with paint markers. Most intense are the dark background colors: black, deep blue, burgundy, dense green, and purple shades that are in high contrast to the metallic paint markers. White paint markers are also wonderful on dark cardstock. Often evocative of night, the artwork that is inspired by these materials would be difficult to achieve in any other way. It is fascinating to be able to draw light on darkness, and it is also a reversal of usual experience to make distinct controlled lines with paint. Effects can be achieved with paint markers that would be impossible with paint and a brush.

Oil-based markers are also an excellent choice for older children, teens, and adults. The quality of the medium is well worth the investment for durability and for the additional surface applications that could not be accomplished with a water-based medium.

CARDS AS GIFTS

Cards *are* gifts. This is their sole purpose. Card making sessions are all about expressing ideas and emotions with the intention of giving them away. There is nothing quite as endearing or profound as a child's artwork and their own words on a card. No Hallmark item could ever compare.

There is something about card making that appeals to the generosity of children. They approach it with zest and determination. Some make a list of loved ones and make sure everyone gets a unique card. Names are often painstakingly written and envelopes embellished and sealed with triumphant fanfare.

This is all that children really have to give, these private gifts that are heartfelt and handmade. Yes, the drawings are simple, and the words are often misspelled, but the messages are all the more eloquent for their innocence. It is possible that a card made in these art sessions could become a valued heirloom for the distant descendants of the child who made it. These are the types of things that are cherished and saved. This is one of the many reasons why quality materials that will endure are offered during these sessions.

The opportunity to make cards is especially welcome close to holidays. But there always seems to be a birthday coming, or someone who needs the message to "get well soon." Adults and teens never seem to hesitate to make cards right along with the younger children. Everyone seems to know someone who would love a handmade card.

Quality cards can be made by simply folding a piece of cardstock in half and placing markers and envelopes nearby. Water-based paint markers can be an exciting addition; just a few metallic and white markers on the table will serve to create dazzling special effects on darker colored cards.

This is the most simple of all art groups. Although little preparation is needed, the art experience has an especially high yield of enjoyment both for those who give the cards and those who have the pleasure of receiving them. Sometimes, the giver and receiver are sitting next to each other at the table. Each will hover over their own "secret" work, promising not to look at the other, until the moment the cards are exchanged and the "surprise" is revealed!

Card making is all about sharing. So be generous with materials and time. This is an example of a group that could last all day long and take place many times a year. Cardstock, envelopes, and washable markers could be placed in the center of a room with a simple sign inviting everyone to take part in making cards.

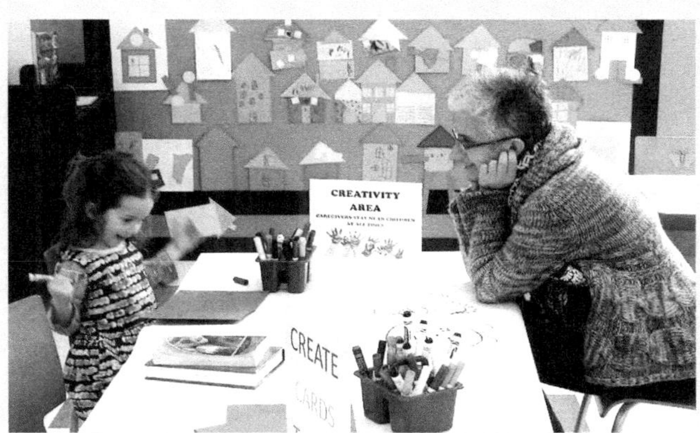

Figure 8.2 Creating cards: Hannah Burgio and Robin Capuano.

DESIGNING CARDS

White and colored cardstock

Fine- and broad-tip markers

Water-based paint markers—including silver, gold, and white

6" × 9" envelopes (optional)

Preparation: Fold cardstock folded in half to 5 ½" × 8 ½".

Make signs for table (optional).

Table Setup: Protect table with a plastic tablecloth and brown craft paper.

Arrange cardstock down the center of the table with an array of colors in reach of each person.

Place markers and paint markers in separate bins, with envelopes nearby.

Place a sign explaining card making and invite taking an envelope for each card (optional).

Guidelines:

Encourage everyone to create at least one card and take envelopes for decorating or sending.

Recommend using paint markers on top of regular markers (not the other way around).

Caution that paint markers will need time to dry before folding cards or placing in envelopes.

Make scissors, glue, and tape available on request.

Special Note: Paint markers are not appropriate for very young children.

Paint markers can be placed on a separate table with a sign advising age restrictions.

Variations: Try printing a frame on the front of the card to emphasize that it is a work of art.

Offer die-cut shapes made from discarded books, sheet music, and old maps to glue on the cards.

Also, offer blank postcards with a template printed on cardstock that meets the guidelines for the USPS. One side will be for the stamp and message, the other side for artwork that can go through the mail.

Near holidays in addition to cards, provide blank paper bags and bookmarks that can be designed with art and given to others.

THE ART OF ADULTS IN OPEN ART STUDIO

When an art studio is open for everyone, adults are full participants. They are not simply spectators or helpers in a child's group. When we first meet adults in the art studio, they usually come as the caregivers of young children. They are the parents, grandparents, nannies, and neighbors. It is not unusual for a child to dash into the room, find a place at the table, and begin exploring the art materials before the caregiver has even stepped through the door. Some adults may even attempt to "drop off" a very young child, and only remain because it has been made clear that it is necessary to stay. So how do we make it inviting for adults to participate? When our signs affirm that this is a place where *everyone* can make art, some adults are pleasantly surprised and eagerly take a place beside the children. Others will be reticent to sit down and noticeably uncomfortable at the art table. Some reach for their phones only to discover the sign that is a "screen-free zone." Now, they really look lost. This is a point where some intervention is needed.

Just because each place at the art table has been set for everyone to participate, it still may not be evident to the adult newcomer. So say it outright, "This is for you!" This invitation will be enough for some, others will need more from us. Inevitably comes the reasoning, "I'm just not creative." Respond by saying, "Just try the art materials. You don't need to make anything at all . . . just have fun. . . " This permission to be playful with art has long been missing for most adults. Many buried their creative spirit under the weight of adult responsibilities. "I really don't have time . . . I really shouldn't be spending my time just doing this. Art materials are wasted on me." The "not creative" myth has been internalized long ago and has become a self-fulfilling prophecy, stopping them before they start. We now give permission to begin again.

This reassurance is effective because it is essentially permission to fail—to not make anything—and to enjoy doing nothing noteworthy at all! Once the pressure is off to succeed, no one needs to impress anyone else. It is okay to mess around, take risks, and experiment. Then it becomes possible to tap back into the childlike curiosity that leads to marvelous discoveries and wondrous adventures. Given this chance, these adults are often the last ones to leave the art studio. They say things like this: "I've not felt so creative since I was a child!"

The examples of artwork in Figure 8.3 were created by adults with oil pastel in the Open Art Studio.

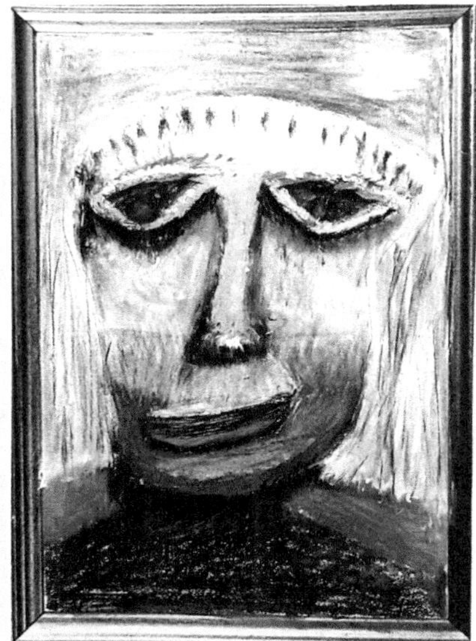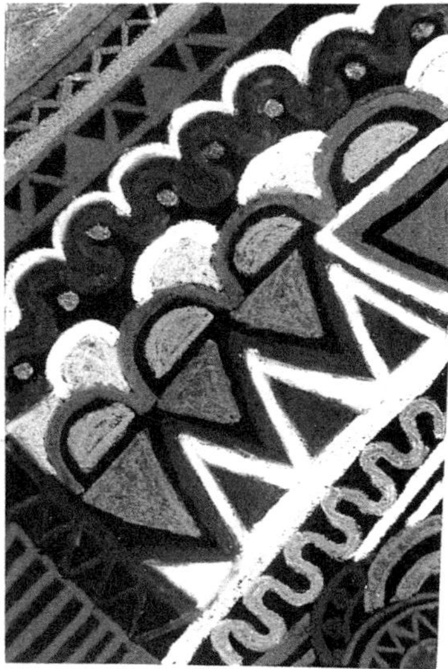

Figure 8.3   Artwork by Scot M. Andersen and MahaRajini Krishnan.

OIL PASTELS

White, black, or dark-blue cardstock sheets measuring 8½" × 5½"

Nontoxic oil pastels

Paper towels

Preparation: Cut 8½" × 11" sheets in half to make 8½" × 5½" pieces.

Cover tables with brown craft paper to protect surfaces.

Table Setup: Place one dark and one light piece of 8½" × 5½" paper with 12 oil pastels on a folded paper towel at each place at the table.

Display a sign describing oil pastel techniques (optional).

Guidelines: Invite participants to experiment with the colors on the different background papers.

Mention that it can be like day and night (optional).

Explain that colors can be layered and blended.

Offer more paper as needed.

Special Note: Oil pastels are softer than crayons and the colors are more vibrant. They are easier to apply but can also easily break into small pieces. Oil pastels are not recommended for children under the age of three and those who may put them in their mouth.

Variations: On watercolor paper or cardstock, oil pastels can be blended by using a cotton swab dipped in baby oil for a softened painterly effect.

Print frames on cardstock for miniature works of art using oil pastels blended with baby oil (also use these frames for sessions with other art media). Print many types of small frames and design a "museum" wall with tiny works of art! Or cut reversible small frames to be hung as aspects of a mobile.

COLLAGE AS ART

The word *collage* comes from the French word *coller,* meaning "to gum." According to the *Concise Oxford Dictionary of Art Terms,* collage is "a pictorial technique in which pieces of cut paper of all shapes and types are combined and stuck down on to another surface to create a design. Already popular with children and amateurs, it was taken up by major artists in the early 20th century beginning with the Cubists."

Georges Braque, Pablo Picasso, and Juan Gris led the way in the Cubist movement to push the boundaries of art that confined them in the early 20th century. By going beyond the limitation of paint, the artist's canvas also became a surface for gluing objects. This was a daring concept intended to be rebellious, satirical, aimed to startle the viewer, and, ultimately, to provoke questions about the definition of fine art.

Brandon Taylor, a professor of art history at the University of Southampton, has written extensively about collage as an art form. He recounted that "collage deliberately evoked the cognitive and technical standards of the child, the playful, or the mad—suggesting that anyone can shape material in this way, that anyone can practise in the field of the fine arts" (Taylor 2004, 9).

It was an astonishing idea to use discarded debris to create art worthy of a museum! Ordinary clippings, tickets, labels, postage stamps, song sheets, and wallpaper patterns—and an array of other fragments—were selected and arranged in such a way that they were no longer mundane or useless but valued for the ability to amaze the eye and challenge the viewer to see anew. Collage became an art form, and these visual statements could not be expressed as effectively in any other way.

Most basically, the term *collage* refers to pieces of paper glued onto a flat surface. If these are pictorial images or photographs, it is a *montage* or *photomontage.* If the work is three-dimensional and includes objects, it is an *assemblage.* The word collage has come into common usage to include all these variations. So it is in the broadest sense of the term that the word "collage" will be used here.

There is something so seemingly simple about making a collage, and yet the cumulative results can take us by surprise. Because it is a process that often can move forward without a plan, one choice leads to another. Pieces come together, interact, or overlap. Pieces may be aligned in harmony, balanced in asymmetry, pop up off the surface, or stray precariously over the edge.

For a very young child, the simple acts of selecting, placing, and gluing pieces down will be an engrossing process. Through experimentation, they naturally learn to master the essential skill of gluing while having a wonderful time. But why does collage have such appeal for all ages? Perhaps the enticement is the belief that *anyone* can do it. Drawing skills are not required at all. So it becomes an enjoyable way to focus on design, color, and composition.

Older children, teens, and adults, who may be reluctant to take part in other art experiences, tend to give collage a try. Once they begin, they often become deeply engaged in the process and work silently and deliberately for long periods of time. Then they want to make another one! It is captivating to find how the collaged elements interact in unexpected ways. These chance discoveries lead the artist onward, following an inner voice that keeps inquiring, "What will happen if I place this here. . . ?" Even with precut pieces, there are so many options: size, shape, color, orientation, and placement. This incremental process gradually becomes cumulative and progressive. The art product is the result of countless decisions made from a myriad of choices all along the way. This gratifying level of choice distinguishes the art of collage from an assembly-type craft. Each individual effort is a unique accomplishment.

Collage making is excellent experience toward the beginning of a series of art group sessions. It is the ideal model of an art group with intergenerational appeal. The types of collage are so varied that even offered once a month, there would be no need for repetition for over a year. Numerous types of collage can be made from the wide variety of tissue available: there is a spectrum of solid colors, swirled colors, and flecked colors, bold and subtly patterned tissues. Tissue comes in precut small geometric, flower, and leaf shapes. But tissue that is torn by the collagist has edges that are more organic, undulating, and capricious forms. Some art tissues are intended to "bleed" when saturated, and the color will seep into the surrounding paper like watercolor, giving a mixed media effect. Each type of tissue is a very different experience. Many shapes and varieties can be offered at once or be selectively combined to focus options.

Tissue can be applied to watercolor paper and many other surfaces using liquid laundry starch as the adhesive. Liquid starch will even adhere tissue to wax paper, resulting in semi-translucency for hanging in a window or on a mobile. Torn or cut tissue can be applied to paper masks, cardboard boxes, or other three-dimensional surfaces. Try it on glass. Make a large-scale collaborative mural on a window using liquid starch to adhere the pieces of tissue.

Collage has the advantage of being inexpensive. Newspapers, wrapping paper, painted paper, discarded books, magazines, old maps, and sheet music are just a few examples of low-cost or free sources for collage materials. Cutting can transform these papers into flowers, birds, and many other shapes that can be incorporated into collage. Better yet, simply provide the scissors, paper, and glue and trust the collagist. The one who makes the art will know the best.

Inspired by the cutouts of Matisse, remnant pieces of colorful cardstock can be pasted on light and dark paper. Gather all the pieces of leftover paper that has been die-cut in the library. Save the scraps that would have been thrown away. Clipped into random pieces, these elegant abstract remnants make collages with a seemingly infinite array of variations. A shape-cutting device opens the options for producing large quantities of interesting scraps. Scissors on the table will further enhance the creative choices. Provide markers, and participants can add designs or details to the abstract shapes that they imagine resemble something else, such as a face in the collage.

Three-dimensional collages, or assemblages, can be made by using tacky glue that dries quickly. Long strips of paper can be twisted, folded, intertwined and then fastened. Surprising effects can be achieved when turning and twisting dual-colored papers that reveal a different color on the reverse side.

Collage with mixed media and further the options by adding objects such as feathers, string, netting, foil, scraps of cloth, and natural found objects.

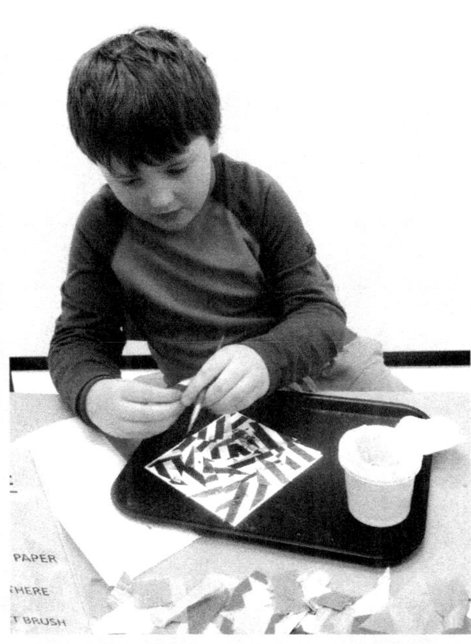

Figure 8.4   Artwork by James Guarnieri-Cruess.

TISSUE COLLAGE

Tissue paper—bleeding (colors run) and/or nonbleeding

Watercolor paper

Liquid starch

No-spill cups with brushes

Plastic trays

Preparation: Protect table with plastic tablecloth and brown craft paper.

Tear tissue in irregular shapes or precut geometric pieces.

Cut watercolor paper into 6" × 6" squares.

Pour a small amount (1/2 inch) of liquid starch into each spill-proof cup.

Table Setup: On each tray, place one piece of paper, a cup with liquid starch, and a brush.

Scatter tissue collage pieces down the center of the table.

Place a sign explaining the art process (recommended).

Guidelines: Explain the process:

First, the brush is used to wet the paper and then the tissue pieces are placed on the paper.

The facilitator may also encourage experimentation with overlapping and layering using more liquid starch to set pieces in place.

Call attention to color mixtures: "What happened when you put yellow tissue over blue?"

Explain that "bleeding" colors run and create watercolor effects.

Variations: Tissue collage can be done with torn tissue, geometric pieces, or precut shapes such as leaves. There are many other surfaces other than watercolor paper for tissue collage: try glass surfaces and bottles, or use wax paper for semitransparent art to display in a window. Collage directly on windows using liquid starch as the adhesive. Use a clear drying glue to collage on foil, plastic, and even discarded CDs for eye-catching effects that can be turned into mobiles. Experiment!

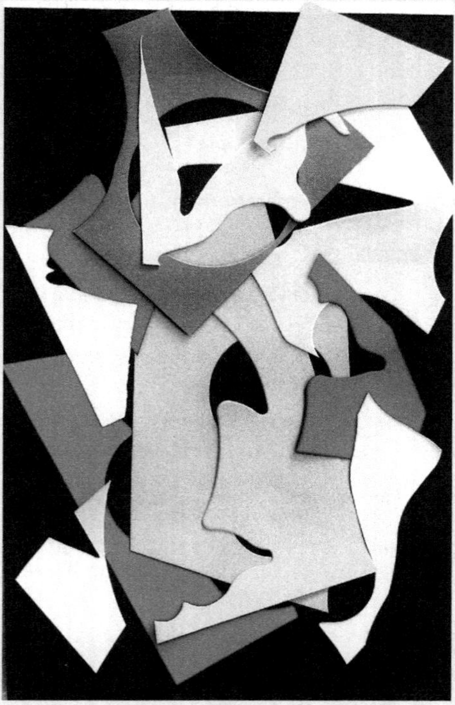

Figure 8.5   Artwork by Maya LeBlond.

REMNANT CARDSTOCK COLLAGES

Black or dark-blue cardstock sheets measuring 8½" × 5½"

White cardstock 8½" × 5½"

Various shapes of cut cardstock—from remnants of other die-cut pieces

White glue sticks

Preparation: Cut 8½" × 11" sheets in half to make 8½" × 5½" pieces of white and black (or dark blue) cardstock for background papers.

Use saved die-cut paper remnants and randomly cut them smaller for collage pieces.

Table Setup: Protect the table with brown craft paper.

Place one dark and one light piece of 8½" × 5½" paper as background for collages.

One glue stick for each person.

Down the center of the table, place all the smaller cut pieces.

Provide a sign explaining the art process.

Display books on the artwork of Matisse nearby (optional).

Guidelines: Invite participants to make at least one light and one dark background collage. Pieces can be placed flat, layered, or bent for 3-D effects.

Encourage experimentation.

Offer more background paper as needed.

Provide scissors, staplers, tape, and markers on request or place in a nearby accessible area.

Variations: Select a limited palette of colors, such as black and white cardstock on red paper. Provide a range of colorful geometric cardstock shapes—circles, squares, triangles—to encourage shape and color identification with younger participants.

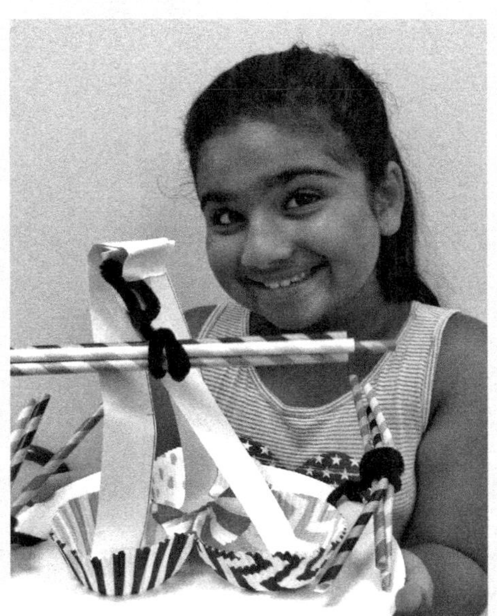

Figure 8.6   Artwork by Manya Trivedi.

3-D Collage

Patterned gift wrap, paper straws, muffin paper-baking cups, paper straws, 3-ounce paper cups, chenille stems, paper towel tubes

Cardboard bases

Scissors

White quick-drying glue, tape, staplers, string

Markers (optional)

Preparation: Place some of the tools and materials onto a cart to provide for "extra" needs.

Cut some of the gift wrap into 12" × 12" sections.

Make a sign: "What can you create with these materials?"

Table Setup: Protect the table with plastic tablecloth and brown craft paper.

Arrange cardboard bases for each person at the table.

Down the table center, place gift-wrap sections, muffin cups, straws, chenille stems, paper towel tubes, scissors, white glue, and tape.

Place a sign on the table: What can you create with these materials?

Guidelines: Explain that the cardboard can be used as a base.

Invite participants to combine the materials creatively to construct a 3-D collage.

Explain to adults with young children that they may need to provide assistance to support their children's creative ideas.

Variations: Include other options: buttons, wallpaper samples, fabric scraps, Styrofoam packing materials, cardboard scraps, discarded puzzle pieces, and other odds and ends.

Design crazy critters (include googly eyes and brass fasteners) or wild inventions.

Or offer ideas to inspire imaginative brainstorming: create a playground, a city on another planet, an abstract work of art . . . what else?

Create collages entirely from nature: shells, sticks, pebbles, feathers, and other small objects.

Invite children to bring in their own found objects to assemble.

OPEN GUIDELINES IN THE ART STUDIO: CLAY

Open guidelines are the opposite of "how to" instructions resulting in a specific product such as a pinch pot. Instead, the way is opened for self-guided discovery. If some incentive to touch the clay is needed at first, guide children to hold the clay in their hands: warm it, roll it, soften it, shape it, or take it apart. Better yet, simply say, "Explore your clay in your own way." This encouragement may be all that is needed for a wonderful time.

Demonstrating a technique at the beginning of a session will open up creative possibilities. For air-dry clay, for instance, give a brief demonstration on how to score and adhere clay parts. Also, as needed, you can explain how to stabilize air-dry clay by using internal supports such as toothpicks to reinforce the structure. Children are usually full of imaginative notions and rarely need much assistance to follow through with their plans. There is something especially empowering about fashioning handmade items. The child can experience being the "creator" of a small entity such as a bunny with a carrot or a dragon with dessert. The artwork can become toys. Don't be surprised if the bunny nibbles the carrot and the dragon devours the dessert!

There will be times when one child will show another other how to work through a problem or how to do something new. This can be a powerful learning experience for both of them. This is when a facilitator guides by stepping aside so the children can lead the way. As much as possible, it is our aim to allow children to work through problems without adult intervention and to formulate their own creative solutions, as well as have a chance to learn from one another. Let the children teach you.

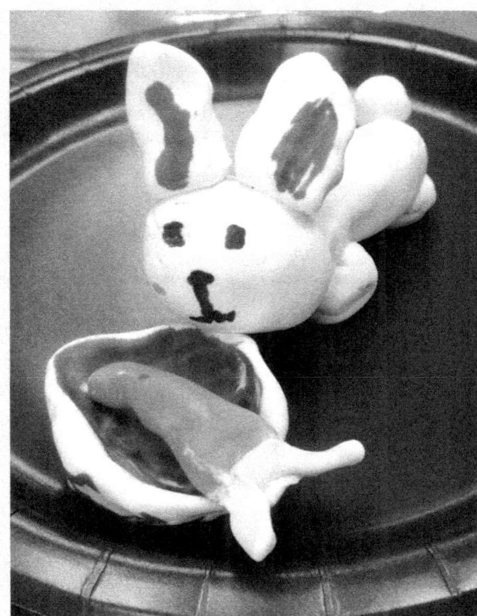

Figure 8.7   Artwork by Grace Earnest.

AIR-DRY MODELING COMPOUND WITH MARKERS

Primary colors and/or white modeling clay

Dark paper plates with water-resistant surface

Washable markers

Modeling tools and rollers (optional)

Plastic bags or wrap to keep clay moist

Preparation: On a dark paper plate, place two ounces of white modeling compound or about ½ ounce each of yellow, blue, red, and white Model Magic® or a similar air-dry clay. Seal inside an individual plastic bag until ready to use.

Make a sign explaining that due to small parts choking hazard, clay and modeling compound are not recommended for children under age three. Direct parents to the other art tables set with materials appropriate for younger children.

Table Setup: Place at each setting a wrapped plate of assorted clay compound with washable markers nearby.

Have clay modeling tools, texture plates, and rollers available on request (optional). Have a sign encouraging exploration and play with the clay: experimentation, mixing, and blending of colors (optional).

Place a sign with age restrictions on the table.

Guidelines: Encourage exploring the texture, squishing, and stretching the clay.

Describe how colors can be mixed to create marbleized effects and that the primary colors can be blended to make secondary colors (optional).

Explain that markers can be used on this clay to add color and detail.

Notes: This art experience is not appropriate for anyone who might place clay in their mouth. Not all air-dry clays are compatible with markers, so please check product specifications. As a commercial product, air-dry modeling clay, dough, or compound can be expensive. Try online recipes for cost effective alternatives.

Variations: There are many types of nontoxic modeling compounds available on the market. Alternate colors are available, such as natural earth tones, pastel, and bright neon. Air-dry modeling clays may also be painted or glazed when dry (check manufacturer's recommendations for suitable glazes). Use toothpicks and/or cut plastic stir sticks as internal support for structures or to add surface detail and textures. Offer items such as feathers and beads to embellish creations.

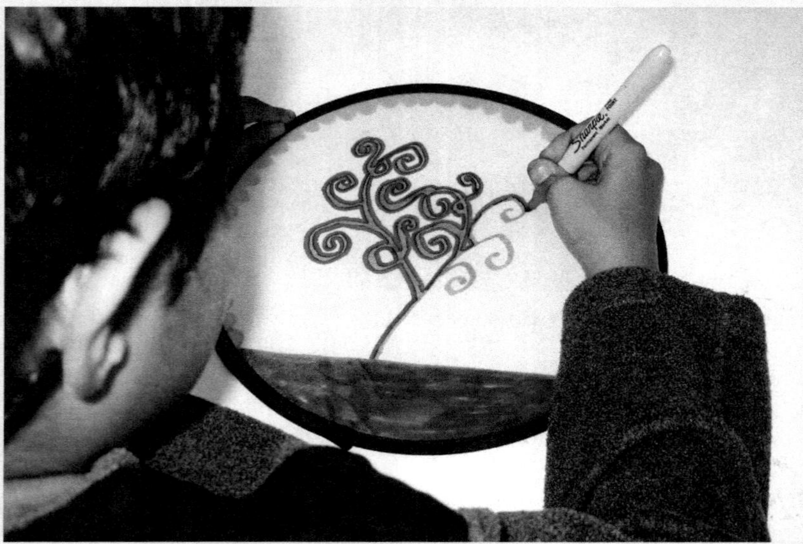

Figure 8.8   Artwork by Vikramaditya Chetnani.

ART ON FLYING DISCS

White or light-color flying fabric discs with storage pockets

Broad- and fine-tip markers (markers not labeled "washable" work best)

Paper towels

Preparation: Make a sign explaining the art process (optional).

Table Setup: Protect the table with a plastic tablecloth and brown craft paper.

Place one flying disc and storage pocket at each place on the table.

Distribute various colors and sizes of markers in bins down the center of the table.

Place sign on the table describing the art process (optional).

Guidelines: Encourage children to design their own disc and storage pocket.

Advise them that the artwork will be reversed on the other side.

Demonstrate how to collapse the disc into the pocket.

Explain that children can have fun throwing the discs, but not inside a building and to never run after a disc into the street.

Special Note: The choice of materials are based on durability for use on the surface of the nonwoven fabric discs. This artwork is also a toy. Markers labeled "washable" may smudge with handling. While permanent markers are the most durable, they are not recommended for young children. Other markers can be used successfully. Markers that are intended for children but do not have the "washable" label are the best choice. Advise caution about clothes. These markers are not as easy to clean up and will require a longer wash time for hands.

Variations: Try crayon texture rubbings on the surface, use dark-colored large unwrapped crayons on the side for most effective transfer of color. These rubbings can be done with texture plates or natural objects such as leaves. Toddlers (as well as older children) enjoy using dot markers on the flying discs.

When we envision a library as the community living room, an art studio will be the area within for gathering and truly being with others. Inclusive and welcoming of all ages and levels of ability, Open Art Studio invites the heightened interaction that occurs with shared experiences. Community families from diverse cultural, racial, and economic backgrounds join in the joy of creating alongside each other. Generations can genuinely interconnect, and time will slow down for the hurried child. A library art studio is more than a place to make art. It is a place to make memories.

9

Groups for Children and Teens

CREATIVE ART GROUPS

Children in Creative Art groups work from inspirations, imagination, and observations as they gain fluency in the language of art. These library art groups designed for elementary-school-age children are open-ended and choice-based to elicit diverse creative responses. Many of the sessions involve the open exploration of art media. Some sessions offer experience with a familiar art material, such as paint. Other sessions offer unusual art materials, such as paint sticks, or a chance to work on an unusual surface, such as tooling foil. Some groups provide the option to work from a theme. These open-ended themes have been inspired by art history, world art, contemporary artists, illustrators, and art for environmental or social causes.

It may seem redundant to say *Creative Art,* but emphasis on the creative process differentiates these groups from arts and crafts activities and from classes teaching art. These Creative Art sessions have been held at the library in the late afternoon during the school year or during the daytime in the summer. Over the years, these exciting and challenging groups have had many configurations. At first, Creative Art was divided into two age groups: kindergarten through third grade and fourth through sixth grade. This proved to be a generally workable guideline that is recommended for facilitators.

In most recent years, however, there has been a merging of these two groups mainly due to staff time constraints. This merging was initially a compromise experiment that has proven to have some surprising advantages. Although in many ways it is more challenging to have such diverse ages, for the most part, it has been remarkably successful. What has happened can be compared to the one-room schoolhouse effect. The younger children tend to admire and learn from the older children, who enjoy this status. Usually, similar ages cluster together, which is also fine. Siblings that would have been in different groups now attend together. Parents have been pleased by the convenience of one group because it fits easily into after school and summer schedules.

It soon became apparent, however, that kindergarteners were too young for this wide age spread. So the group became for children in first through sixth grade. Usually, the majority of children who attend are in grade three, with a few older and younger attendees. Groups during the school year have had about 10 to 12 participants. This number can easily double or triple in the summer.

The word "challenging" is used to describe these groups because they can require the most thought, preparation, and involvement by the facilitator of all art sessions. Because of this, it is advised that a facilitator have a background in art with knowledge of art history as well as contemporary artists and illustrators. Working knowledge of two- and three-dimensional art materials will also be necessary. A facilitator will need to understand how to locate and purchase quality art materials and how to present various art experiences that are age appropriate and conducive to creative choice.

Former art educators will need to unlearn teaching in order to become a facilitator of creativity. It will be disconcerting not to take the lead. But it can be done. Most of all, it is imperative to understand child growth and development and the essential role of art, creativity, and play during childhood. These pages provide an overview of why and how to present choice-based art experiences with school-age children, but further research into theory and practice is recommended before facilitating these groups. Some sources for more information are found in the bibliography, but there are many other books and valuable resources that remain beyond the scope of this preliminary listing.

Creative Art groups can be energizing, fascinating, and fatiguing for the facilitator, who may be challenged by the fast pace of these sessions. Usually well attended by highly creative children, each child will be going their own way. This is exactly what we want, but it may be everything a facilitator can do to keep up. The key will be to enable children to find what they need in the room and work as independently as possible on their own ideas.

Many of these children are attracted to these "extra" art groups because they are already highly motivated to make art. They may have been identified as "creative" or artistically "gifted" by the schools. Some will have already received awards and honors for their artwork. Experienced with a wide range of art materials, they are likely to be well acquainted with a variety of ways to use them. They are interested in experimentation and eager to mix media.

The older children in Creative Art delight in telling others what they know about Impressionism and Surrealism and have strong opinions about this and that period in art history. They can be quite knowledgeable about artists and their techniques, but nearly all these children have had very little experience working from their own ideas. This is what a creative art has to offer. It gives the chance—perhaps one of the few opportunities these children ever have—to work in a group creating art from their own ideas and imagination without anyone insisting they follow adult instructions.

Most of the children in these sessions just simply enjoy doing art and are glad to have a chance to do more of it. A few children, however, are less willingly placed by parents into these groups. Sometimes they come in with an eagerly motivated sibling, who is the designated "artist" in the family. In contrast to this enthusiasm, reluctant artists are often subdued and hesitant to take part in creative experiences and have little confidence in their own ideas. These children may not have always felt this way. "A phenomenon observed across several studies describes a reduction in original thinking in children ages 9–10 years compared with younger and older children—the 'fourth grade slump.' The social pressures on young adolescents toward being part of the crowd often lead children to lose their capacity to think 'out of the box.'" (Hadani and Jaeger 2015, 6).

Children with low confidence will need attention and some gentle guidance to become involved and stay in the art process. Once again, exploration with art materials is the most effective approach, especially in the beginning. As resistance lowers, enthusiasm builds, and they may be surprised to discover the ways art can intersect with their other interests and capabilities. If they appreciate reptiles, drawing or making a clay snake is quite easy. If they decide to add legs, there is a lizard! Children who are reluctant at first often become enthusiastic advocates for the art process. They learn the most. They learn that they are creative too.

A number of children who attend Creative Art are homeschooled, and the library is a primary source for art experiences outside the home. This is also an important place for them to socialize. Very often, homeschooled children do exceptionally well in these groups. They look forward to art, plan their week around the groups, and are especially disappointed when a series of sessions ends.

One homeschooled child, who was reluctant to glue or to paint when she first started coming to the art studio years ago, has since become an avid experimenter and art enthusiast. She loves to entreat other children to create with her. She has remarked, "I never really liked art before I started coming here, I wasn't really very good at it. Now, it's my favorite thing to do. My mom made a creativity table for me at home. I am an artist . . . I may not grow up to *work* as an artist, but I will always love doing it!"

ART MEDIA AND PROCESS

There are many ways to do choice-based Creative Art groups. The simplest and most common approach is to have no theme. The objective is to explore art materials. The main table is set with an invitation to explore and create, and everyone decides their own way. Creative Art groups commonly offer art materials such as markers, oil pastels, collage materials, paint, or clay. Sometimes, supplemental materials and tools are placed at the center of the table to encourage sharing, interaction, and child-led choices without any need for assistance from the facilitator. Sessions can also introduce less familiar materials such as gel sticks, water-soluble pastels, soft pastels, paint sticks, and paint markers. The facilitator begins with a brief explanation of the properties of the art material and encourages children to explore without showing the example of a completed product.

Soft pastels are an art material that is intriguing to explore and can also be the basis for themed works inspired by the approach, techniques, and motivations of various artists. Artworks made with pastels are often referred to as "paintings," and indeed they have a painterly quality that goes beyond drawing. Soft pastels are an exciting medium for larger scale works that can be accomplished in a relatively short time. Distinctly different from oil pastel, the consistency of soft pastels is dry powdery compressed pigment. As always, it important to select nontoxic materials and carefully read labeling instructions. Although not appropriate for younger children, soft pastels are ideal for Creative Art age groups and teens. The colors can be easily layered, smudged, and softened using a blending stump, shaper, or chamois cloth. Toned papers textured for pastel are preferable but can be expensive. The quality of the surface, however, will enhance the experience of working with soft pastels.

Trust that children will catch on quickly to the process. Most do. The few who do not understand at first, soon learn through their own discoveries and from seeing what others around them are doing. When an adult shows an example of a finished *product* to explain a *process*, we limit rather than open up options. This is the opposite of our intention, so we must keep in mind that children are easily impressed and influenced by adult examples. This is how they are taught in school. As a result, children learn to imitate adult models and closely follow their instructions. Children's own ideas are discouraged in schools when they are labeled as going off topic and not following directions.

As facilitators, we must be ever mindful of a child's creative right to choices. The unique perspective and preferences of a child are easy to underestimate and overlook. We need to take care not to block the creative way. A child's inner vision is easily diverted and captivated by an eye-catching adult product. It is confusing to say, "This is my example of what to do, but don't do this. Do your own thing." This is a contradictory statement.

Let the art media alone be the inspiration. Children need to learn how to make their own decisions and follow through with them. But those who have rarely had choice-based experiences will initially be stunned by this level of freedom. They are used to specific directions in school—even in art classes. Some may just stare down at the blank paper or sit motionless before the untouched lump of clay, while others may begin to talk incessantly and avoid doing art for a while. A few might ask for help by saying, "Tell me what you want me to do." This is a challenge to resist; it would be tempting to rush in and "fix" this uneasiness by giving directions to make something simple. This, however, would not be encouraging creative thinking or self-reliance.

From the beginning, a facilitator needs to show trust in the child's ability to make creative decisions. The question can be reversed: "What do you want to do?" Usually by this time, other children who have become familiar with choice-based groups will add, "You can do whatever you want in here!" Looking around, it will soon become apparent that everyone is working from their own ideas. The artwork in progress by the children in the studio serves as the "example" of diverse responses. This is usually incentive enough for the reluctant child to move forward with an idea.

Sometimes, however, this is not enough. If additional support is needed, it is best to start with simple suggestions that open up inquiry, entice exploration, and invite discovery. If it is clay, a child can find out what happens if the clay is pushed down flat or if the clay is rolled long or formed into a ball. Once these options have been tried, the child may realize that these are the basic elements for creating representational objects, if they *choose* to do so. Of course, it is not necessary to make anything at all.

A facilitator often uses words that advocate for curiosity and independent thinking, such as *explore.* Yet there are other words that are even more effective with older children, such as *investigate* and *experiment.* These terms call attention to the scientific aspects of art and spark even more ideas for methodical minds. What else can be done with clay? Bend it, twist it, and pull it apart. Let each child come up with ideas and put them into action.

Myriad possibilities open up by offering clay tools, such as rolling pins. Incising and texturing implements can cut into clay or make marks (plastic knives and forks are excellent and inexpensive tools for clay). Keep in mind, however, that once clay tools are placed on the table, everyone will want to try them. Hand building may stop entirely while the group explores the tools. So weigh this carefully before offering them on the table. If the goal is to introduce young children to the qualities of clay and to lower tactile defenses against touching it, then it is best not to place any tools on the table. By the time children are in Creative Art groups, however, they have generally had considerable experience with clay. Still, it is best not to start off with numerous tools that can divert attention away from forming original ideas and carrying through with intentions. Once again, simplicity is key. Tools can be added as needed (or requested) just one at a time. For instance, a child might ask for a tool to make impressions into clay to indicate scales on a dragon. This way, a tool can assist in effectively working through with ideas.

OPEN-ENDED AND INCOMPLETE

The renowned art educator and artist Robert Henri once said, "No work of art is really ever finished. They only stop at good places" (Henri 2007, 177).

Completion of artwork is never required in creative art groups. If we truly believe in placing emphasis on the process, then we need to be consistent about this. To reinforce the value of process, a facilitator can request to take photographs while everyone is still working, and not just focus on finished products. At the end of the session, rather than inquiring "What did you make today?" support the exploratory process by asking instead, "What did you find out today?" This can open up a long list of discoveries that children gleefully share.

Facilitators will constantly bear in mind that products do not need to be made in process groups. When we let go of this need, so will others. Yet this is not easy to do. We could inadvertently be pushing for products. This is especially true when we give time warnings: "Okay, everybody, you have five minutes to hurry up and finish your artwork before we clean up." Instead, say this: "In five minutes we will put away the art materials . . . You will take what you are working on home with you."

A younger child who is a beginner with clay especially needs to be reassured (and so do the parents) that the clay is for exploration and continued experimentation. At the end of the group, wrap the unformed clay tightly and send it with the child to encourage further experience with the clay at home.

Also, children who become engrossed in creating something elaborate and do not finish on time need to know that there is absolutely nothing wrong with this. Children should not be pressured to go faster to finish an art project if the rationale of creativity programming is to cultivate curiosity and to support a deep investment in the process. If it is our objective to validate effort, then when considerable time has been invested, we can reinforce this accomplishment by respecting it. We can ask permission to photograph artwork that is still in process and give encouragement to continue the work at home.

If art materials such as paint markers have been used that are not available at home, the facilitator might choose to be flexible and allow the child to stay in the art studio to work past the usual time. If this extended time is offered, of course there would need to be agreement on the part of the child, the caregiver, and the facilitator. A variation of this plan would be to continue the artwork outside the art room on a table in the library set up with a few art materials. But if a child cannot stay, then the suggestion could be made for the child to continue the work as a "mixed media" project with materials that are at home.

There can also be the option to bring unfinished artwork back to the next art session. This is, of course, dependent on whether the facilitator has the flexibility to make these materials available again during the following session.

INSPIRING SURFACES

Creative art groups can also work on inspiring surfaces. An example of such a surface is tooling foil. A session such as this can begin with a brief talk by the facilitator explaining how a stylus can press into the foil and permanent markers can be used to color the surface. No example of a finished product need be shown.

Just for fun, ask the makers of 3-D printed objects if they would like to paint their objects in the art studio. Because acrylic paints work best on these surfaces, this session would be most suitable for older children (teens and adults may also be invited for a special session). If there are any long-abandoned "orphaned" objects from the printer, these might be made available for painting too. Give it a try!

Other inspiring surfaces in Creative Art include: masks, discarded CDs, fabric flying discs, small cardboard gift boxes, discarded book pages, old maps, and sheet music. Calendars with blank space for art are just right for a winter session. Empty frames printed on full paper—or on half the paper for folded cards—are always an invitation for open-ended art. Making small books will inspire creative writing and illustration.

A variety of art media can be applied to these inspiring surfaces. Choices can be placed on the same table. For example, offer both colored pencils and markers for work on small books. Whenever possible, open up the options with compatible mixed media. When the art materials are incompatible, however, set each choice on a separate table. For example, when creating paper masks, paint markers and glued tissue collage materials would be kept apart as either-or options on different tables. As always, art materials are supplied along with guidelines for their respectful use and care, but the ideas of how to create on these inspiring surfaces will be supplied by the child.

CREATIVITY AND LIMITS

Facilitating creativity means opening up possibilities while setting the margins for freedom. Limitless alternatives will pose a paradox. Endless possibilities are a hindrance that can stop us all in our tracks. A creative block may not be a lack of ideas but the loss of ideas crushed under the weight of overwhelming choices. Once we admit this is true, we would be able to understand that guidelines are essential to the creative process.

Existential psychologist Rollo May explains, "Limits are not only unavoidable in human life, they are also valuable. . . *creativity itself requires limits*, for the creative act arises out of the struggle of human beings with and against that which limits them" (May 1975, 116). He contends,

> Confronting limits for the human personality actually turns out to be *expansive. Limiting and expanding* thus go together . . . the struggle with limits is actually the source of creative productions. The limits are as necessary as those provided by the banks of a river, without which the water would be dispersed on the earth and there would be no river. . . . Creativity arises out of the tension between spontaneity and limitations, the latter (like the river banks) forcing the spontaneity into the various forms which are essential to the work of art or poem. (May 1975, 118–119)

OPEN-ENDED THEMES

What is an open-ended theme? The themes for Creative Art are concepts intended to focus ideas in order to expand possibilities. Just as art materials open the way for imaginative explorations, themed groups offer inspirations that extend a child's repertoire of ideas and range of imagination. Because themed Creative Art groups begin with a brief explanation of the idea by the facilitator, an array of art and illustrations from children's books can be shown to inspire children's ideas and interpretations. There are no step-by-step instructions, just some art materials and an inspiring general idea. Choosing how to use the inspiration requires quite a bit of choice-making all along the way, so each outcome will be unique.

There are some art experiences intended to spark imaginative thought. Similar to cloud gazing in which images are envisioned such as castles and dragons, children can use their imaginations to find and define imagery in scribbles or in textures of paint. Also, children can play a fun group interactive game in which each child draws a simple squiggly line and then gives it to another child, who will then imagine how to develop that line into a drawing.

Themed creativity groups will offer an array of possible ways to be inspired, and from this, children will set their own trajectory to go in a direction of their own. Themes can be found in the art around the world: Aboriginal art, African masks, Russian lacquer boxes, Chinese brush paintings, mandalas, and so on. Themed sessions can follow the history of art starting with cave paintings, ancient Egyptian masks, illuminated manuscripts, da Vinci inventions, and so on. Children can be inspired to create wall murals, paint masks, illuminate initials, and design inventions to make the world a better place.

With the theme in Creative Art of the illuminated initial, for instance, books were briefly shown with photographs of actual medieval manuscripts. The first enlarged letters were intricately detailed and illuminated with gold. Children were invited to make a work of art using their own initial (or any letter). Paint markers including gold and silver were used on a choice of cardstock colors. On and around their initials, children placed symbols and designs that were significant to them. The resulting illuminated initials were strikingly individual and meaningful to each child. After sharing their art with the group, several children mentioned they planned to hang their initials in their rooms.

It is rare that a child will choose not to follow the inspiration and create at least one work based on the theme. Sometimes children go on to make a second and third work centered on the same idea, such as gift initials for relatives. Usually, however, the art goes in another direction. For instance, a child may make an illuminated initial with designs and symbols that interest him, such as planets and stars. When it is completed, he may decide to take another dark piece of paper and use the luminous metallic markers to draw a spaceship landing on another planet with aliens approaching! This ability to freely take a bounding leap of imagination is *creative* art.

Many children this age are now interested in drawing from their own observations and so the choice to work from still life, natural objects, or to draw from photographs is always an option in the art studio. Books on art are readily available nearby for everyone's use in the studio. These shelves hold books on the history of art, artists, illustrators, art media, and various techniques. The majority were collected from books discarded from the library collection, and the others were donated books. There is also a selection of illustrated children's stories and some volumes on nature photography. None of these books circulate. Since there are few concerns about damage, they can be freely browsed for inspiration in the art studio.

Although there are instructional art books available, themed Creative Art groups offer inspiring ideas without specific how-to instructions. The open-ended ideas are simple but expansive to invite diverse interpretations. *Always* the children are offered the option to take part in the theme or not. Because this is not school, art making is an invitation, not an expectation. Children can choose to decline the theme and work entirely on their own ideas.

Children may use the materials set for the theme at the main table or use other art materials at another table. This second table in the studio is set with simple materials: pencils, markers, paper, scissors, and tape. This is an alternative table. Although children can choose to sit there from the beginning of the session, this hardly ever happens. Usually, children go to the alternative table after they finish with the artwork on the main table. At the second table, they work exclusively from their own ideas using familiar materials, such as markers. Here they make self-portraits, landscapes, space battles, whatever comes to mind. The children frequently use this place and time to "teach" each other what they know, such as how to make an origami butterfly or a pop-up card.

INSPIRING THEMES

The question may arise, is providing a theme contrary to creativity? Are we giving examples to copy? No. This is not the same as showing one example of a finished product made by an adult instructor. Why not? Because themes offer a wide array of ideas that open up possibilities rather than narrow them down. Artists will always be inspired by the work of other artists. Children are curious to explore these ideas and interpret them in their own way. There is nothing wrong with this. It is how artists learn.

Themed art groups are at the intersection of art exploration and art education. Children in Creative Art groups are developmentally ready to take part in these experiences. When presented in an inviting way, children are eager to learn from history and the world around them. In one art session inspired by da Vinci's drawings of inventions, the children considered how to make the world a better place and devoted their ingenuity to inventing their own devices. Drawn with markers on large paper, the resulting inventions included a flying parachute machine that produced and transported free food to people in need, an elaborate habitat for turtles, an intricate anti-pollution device for major cities, and an energy source ignited by a hamster running on a wheel!

Da Vinci, Cézanne, Gauguin, Miró, Chagall, Matisse, and Picasso are just a few masters that have influenced painted artwork in these sessions.

The medium of soft pastel was especially suited for works inspired by artists such as Mary Cassatt, Edgar Degas, and Georgia O'Keeffe.

M. C. Escher inspired imaginative intricate marker drawings and Alexander Calder's works led to the construction of innovative mobiles and stabiles. The artwork of Magritte and Dali and other surrealists inspired imaginative and playful juxtapositions as the children depicted everyday objects drawn in surprising contexts, such as a giant shoe playground.

The intent is not to copy the work of a master artist but to glimpse the world through their eyes. To see through the eyes of Georgia O'Keeffe, for instance, as she gazed closely at small flowers while she painted on a grand scale. Children in Creative Art are offered a wide array of natural objects as a starting point but can choose to draw an enlargement of anything. This enables them to see at a deeper level and to convey that vision to others. This leads to discussions of how changes in distance and perspective help us all to see in new ways.

Open-ended themes have also invited participants to be inspired by the motivations and methods of illustrators. Beatrix Potter, Eric Carle, Leo Lionni, David Wiesner, Maurice Sendak, Chris Van Allsburg, Jan Brett, Ezra Jack Keats, Mo Willems, Bill Watterson, and Raina Telgemeier are among the many illustrators, cartoonists, and graphic artists whose artwork has influenced creative art sessions.

Children and teens are also motivated to create art for social and environmental causes and genuinely want to know how to make a difference. It is all too easy to grow up feeling helplessly overwhelmed by the lack of justice in this world. Art can be an influential means of expression. It is possible to raise awareness through persuasive visual statements in support of causes. With a simple and sincere perspective on complex issues, the innocence of the young goes straight to the heart of the matter. Their honesty and compassion has the power to awaken adults who have become disillusioned and desensitized by a never-ending onslaught of negative news. Children have not yet lost trust that the world can change for the better. It is important that they keep this optimism and spirit of activism. Art inspires hope.

> I have just three things to teach: simplicity, patience, compassion.
>
> —Lao Tzu, *Tao Te Ching*, Chapter 67

PROVIDING GUIDANCE WITHOUT LEADING THE WAY

At some time during a series of creative art sessions, a child will inevitably ask for assistance on how to draw more realistically. As they grow older, many children become less comfortable with choice-making and less confident in their abilities. This is a challenge for the facilitator to decide how much intervention is needed and when it becomes intrusive. The simple answer is to use your judgment. But if you must err, err on the side of doing less rather than more.

As it is often the case with children, they ask for less than we think. Just as when a young child asks, "Where do babies come from?" Too often adults overthink the question and can easily say more than is necessary. A good standard would be to first have the child specify exactly what they need from you. It may be quite simple.

An urgent plea, "Help me draw trees!" does not translate to "Draw trees for me!" It may translate as "Help me *visualize* how to draw trees so I can draw them from now on." A child can learn how to mentally "see" a tree and describe it with both words and lines. They can also learn to search books for trees or simply look outside and draw what they see. They can learn to see basic shapes and their relationship to one another and evaluate relative size. They can learn to notice and render light and shadow and texture. There are many ways to facilitate learning to draw, without circumventing the creative process by directing children to copy.

It is not our job to remove impediments or lead the way around challenges. Instead, we encourage children to try out different strategies to solve problems and overcome obstacles on their own. This way, the solution belongs to them, and the accomplishment is their own.

Facilitators need to understand and accept that feelings of disequilibrium are part of the creative process. This is how it feels when things are going *right*. Creativity is not always easy, nor is it comfortable. It can be downright scary. There is treacherous territory ahead. This is the creative edge. The very real possibility of failure is always there. Yet if we provide the support to push onward, not retreat to safety and give up, then valuable territory can be gained from encountering problems.

If there is anything that a creativity facilitator teaches, it is the way for a child to become increasingly independent and self-reliant. The more we succeed, the less we will be needed. To borrow from an old saying, a starving person needs more than just a fish; they need to learn how to fish. People need more than bread and fruit; they need to know how to sow grain and plant orchards. Although quick answers are easy, they rarely have long-term benefits. It takes patience and an investment in time to nurture and cultivate creative resources.

When facilitators model patience and trust the process, children's own decisions direct the way. Open-ended themes are always based on choices. When encountering the blank page, it takes time for children to peer past the white wall of empty space to imagine possibilities there. It takes time to sort through it all and formulate ideas of their own. First, they must face not knowing the answer yet. Then they must decide not to give up. When children learn to keep trying, they learn to persist and navigate onward where curiosity leads them. Then options will open up for exploration and the chance to make meaningful discoveries. This is time well spent that leads to gaining the confidence to try something challenging next time. Learning that independent endeavors are worthwhile, children become more self-reliant. No one can give this to them; they must find it on their own.

TAKING CREATIVE RISKS

When we are on the creative edge, we are no longer safely tucked inside our comfort zone.

When we challenge ourselves, it can be almost as frightening as it is exhilarating. Away from our familiar routine and off the beaten path, we climb just a little higher and go a little further than ever before. We know we are really getting somewhere new when it feels precarious and uncertain. Edgy. Creative people search for this place, not always finding it. There is no certain way. Once there, no one knows how long they can stay. There is always the risk of losing the ground that had been gained. Sometimes we go the wrong way and discover this is not where we belong. Things can get worse before they get better. This adds to the tension and excitement.

It is necessary to feel frightened in order to be courageous. When risks are taken, no one can be quite sure what will happen next. This is the nature of risks. If we know what will happen, then no risk is being taken. It is only by pushing the edge of the known outward that we encounter the unexpected outcome. This is our *uncomfortable* zone. The anxious feelings on the creative edge are intrinsic to the experience. We as facilitators need to understand that uncertainty is not a feeling to be "fixed."

> Not-knowing is true knowledge.
>
> —Lao Tzu, *Tao Te Ching*,
> Chapter 71

If we consistently teach children to expect us to resolve their feelings of uncertainty and solve their problems, they will learn to be dependent on us to lead the way. They will make the decision *not* to be creative and avoid the challenges of choice. It is much easier to follow someone else's ideas than to risk acting on your own.

Being unsure is integral to being creative and not to be avoided; if we felt sure, we would not be on untested ground. Feelings of uncertainty come from encountering the vast array of choices before us. We can see past the filters that normally narrow our vision when our defensive shields are down.

Suddenly we understand. It is not that we have no idea what to do. It is that our options are so limitless that it is overwhelming. But this is exactly what we need to encounter to see enough to go forward on our own way. If someone comes to our "rescue," leading us back to a safe place, then we are following *their* path, not our own. The more we do this, instead of making our own choices, the less confident we will become about our own ability to make problem-solving decisions. Someone else will be expected to always solve our problems for us.

Facilitators will also feel uneasy. It is difficult to resist the urge to give specific directions and quick solutions for problems. This would make everyone feel better for the moment. It would be the easy way. But it would not be the way to creativity.

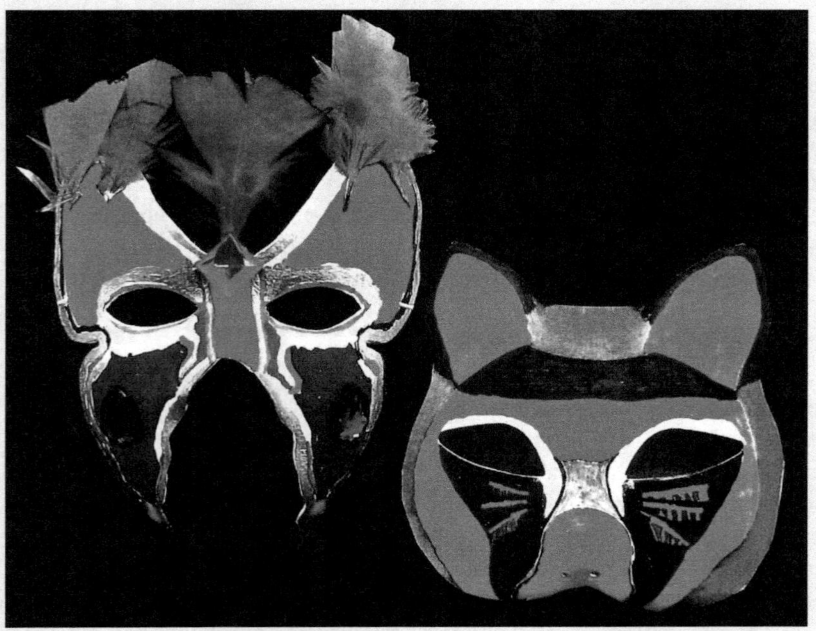

Figure 9.1   Artwork by Acadia Verge and Vikramaditya Chetnani.

MASKS

White pre-shaped paperboard masks: human, butterfly, cat, or various other types

Permanent markers, paint markers, or paint sticks

Preparation: Make a sign explaining the art process (optional).

Table Setup: Protect the table with a plastic tablecloth and brown craft paper.

Place a selection of masks down the center of the table.

Place either permanent markers, paint markers, or paint sticks on the table.

Guidelines: Show many examples of masks from various cultures made throughout history (optional).

Encourage participants to design a unique mask.

Explain whether the masks are intended only for display or if they can be worn.

Special Note: Check manufacturer guidelines whether masks are intended to be worn. Check for proper ventilation holes for breathing. Make sure that elastic bands are sized properly and that vision is not obstructed.

During setup, select only one option per table: permanent markers, paint markers, or paint sticks (including metallic and fluorescent colors). These materials do not mix well with one another. If more than one table is available, separate the art materials and allow a choice between options.

Variations: Washable markers may also be used on the masks. Also try tissue collage with glue sticks or offer embellishments such as feathers and plastic jewels with quick grab glue.

In addition to the above, or with younger children, try superhero paper half masks. Washable markers will work well to make each a unique creation. These inexpensive paper half masks have precut eyes and elastic bands so they can be worn by children.

CIRCLE ART

8 ½" × 8 ½" cardstock (dark color or black)

Various colors of water-based paint markers, including white, silver, and gold

Preparation: Draw a light circle with pencil, or cut out a circle from dark cardstock.

Bring in examples of mandala art and other circular art such as labyrinths. Include deep space and nature photography of circles and spiral forms (optional).

Table Setup: Protect the table with a plastic tablecloth and brown craft paper.

Place a variety of colors of cardstock down the center of the table.

Put pencils and markers near each place setting.

Guidelines: Briefly discuss the history of the mandala and other art inspired by circles. Extend thoughts to circular forms in our surrounding environment and across the universe (optional).

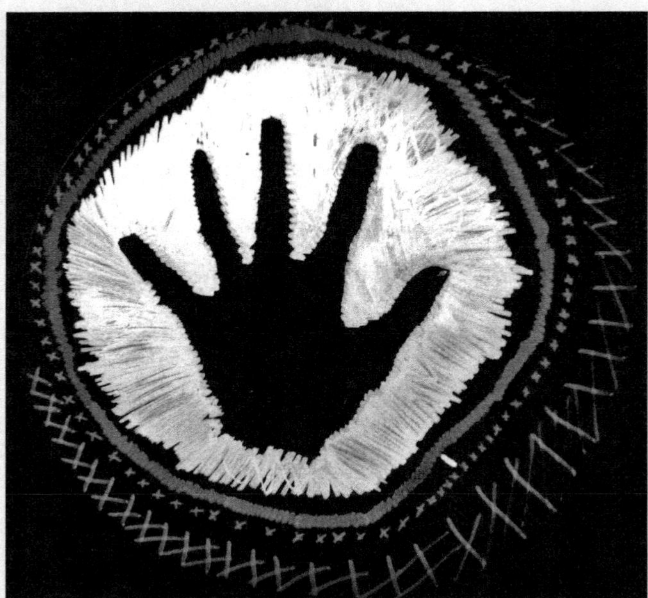

Figure 9.2   Artwork by Sarah Lancaster.

Invite participants to use the circle as the basis for their own artwork.

Encourage choosing symbols that are meaningful to the individual.

Share the results with the group.

Special Note: This art experience will yield a wide array of responses. It is a vivid example of providing a limitation that opens up possibilities.

Variations: Oil or soft pastels can be used instead of paint markers. This art may also be created on metal tooling foil sheets. The experience can be adapted for all ages by offering white liquid tempera paint on a black precut circle.

Story Art

Cardstock various colors

Metallic gel crayons or Stabilo Woody 3-in-1 colored pencils

Scissors, tape, glue sticks

Table Setup: Protect table surfaces with paper. Place art media and various papers down the center of the table.

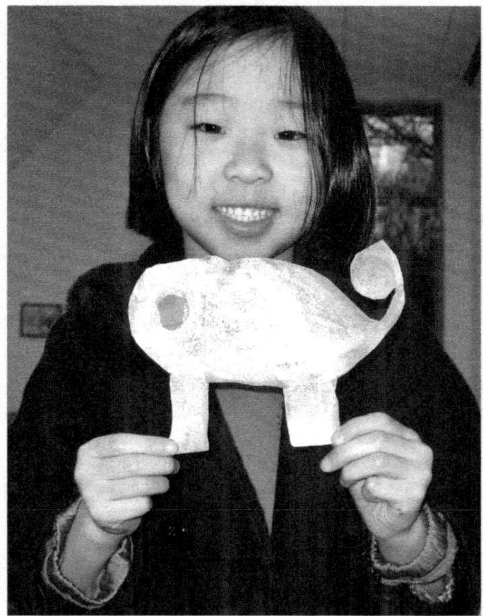

Figure 9.3   Artwork by Anna Chung. Photograph by Megan Grosch.

Procedure: Read a classic picture book that inspires art such as Leo Lionni's *A Color of His Own* or Eric Carle's *The Mixed-Up Chameleon.*

Children design their own story character or creature and tell their story to others.

Variations: This art experience can be done with endless variations of stories and art media.

Standing creatures can be made by designing them on folded paper and cutting out double to make four legs. Alternatively, paper stands can be added with slots or with tabs glued on bases.

Children can also perform stories in which the characters interact with each other.

This is a way to organize this in a group: One child starts the story by talking about their character, each child in turn adds to the narrative by saying, "... and *then* along came a . . ." and describing their character and what happens next!

BOOKS

A booklet stapler (recommended method) or a manual comb-binding machine with ¼ inch comb-binding spines (box of 100—white)

White cardstock, pencils with erasers, colored pencils, and markers

Preparation: Cut white cardstock into 8½" × 5½" sheets.

Booklet stapler method: Fold the cut sheets in half, and staple in the crease for small books.

Binding machine method: Cut the sheets to make 5½" × 4¼" pages, and bind on the long edge.

Trim excess binding spine with scissors (save extra for making tiny books later).

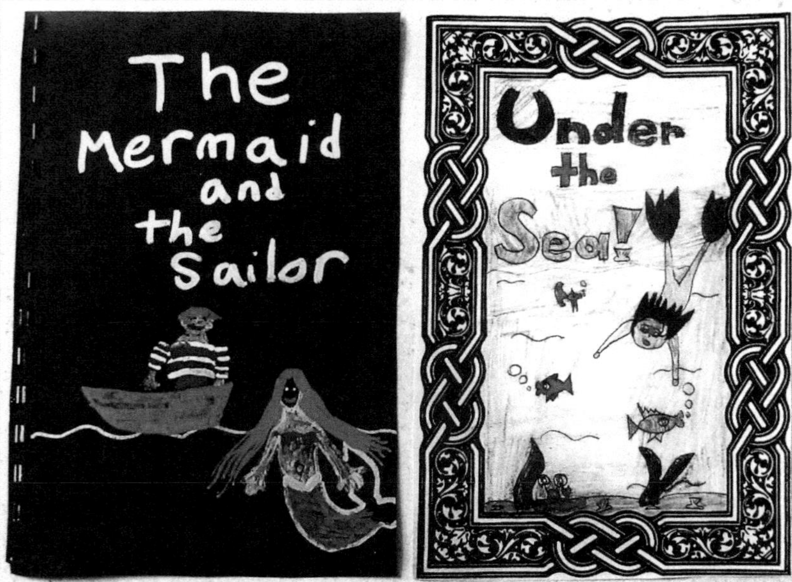

Figure 9.4   Book cover art by Natalie Kay Ith and Abhirami Srivel.

Make 8 to 10 pages in each book.

Prepare more than one book for each participant.

Table Setup: Cover the table with brown craft paper to protect the surface.

Place a book at each setting.

Place markers and pencils in bins on the table.

Guidelines: Explain that each participant will be the author and illustrator of a book. Remember to design a cover and be mindful of how the pages will be used (pencils are available to plan ahead). Use imagination! Stories and illustrations are shared at the end of the group.

Special Note: Allow a minimum of one hour for this group. Some participants may not finish; others may have time to complete more than one book.

Variations: Print a variety of empty borders on the front covers. Provide books of alternative colors, such as all black books or mixed half black and half white (with paint markers for the dark paper) to inspire stories about day and night. Provide alterative book sizes. Tiny books are charming and especially appealing when offered as a second book (or a take home book for later).

If possible, allow time for the children take part in the book-binding process.

Do a series of sessions based on illustrations inspired by wordless picture books or Caldecott Award illustrators. Children can create their own nonfiction books: dinosaurs, ballet, sports, whatever inspires them.

The sky is not the limit—go beyond! Create an outer space saga. Devise an ancient history mystery or futuristic fairy tale! Write and illustrate a poem or a memory. Create shaped books, see-through books, lift-the-flap, or pop-up books.

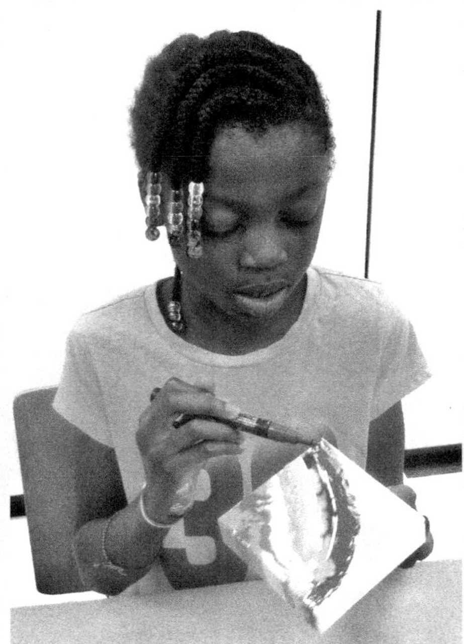

Figure 9.5 Artwork by Sasha Mensah.

ART ON BOXES

White, brown, and black small gift boxes with lids—square and rectangular

Paint markers

Preparation: Research decorative art on boxes, including Russian lacquer boxes depicting traditional Russian fairy tales (optional).

Table Setup: Protect the table with a plastic tablecloth and brown craft paper.

Place a variety of color, sizes, and shapes of boxes down the center of the table.

Separated into bins, place a variety of paint markers, including white, silver and gold.

Guidelines: Display a wide variety of art that is made on boxes with a few historical examples of Russian lacquer boxes with fairytale inspiration (optional).

Ask participants to choose a small cardboard box to decorate with their own artwork and ideas. Remind that the boxes may also be decorated inside.

Encourage creating a second box that may be the same or a different color and size.

Share the results with the group.

Sample questions include: Do you plan to give your box as a gift or keep it for yourself? If you plan to put something inside, what will it be?

Variations: Try other colors of small boxes (including silver and gold).

Offer larger white folded boxes (working on them unassembled). Use a box template to cut and fold boxes.

Create "Story Boxes" and share the stories with the group.

Use permanent markers.

Try collage materials and mixed media on boxes.

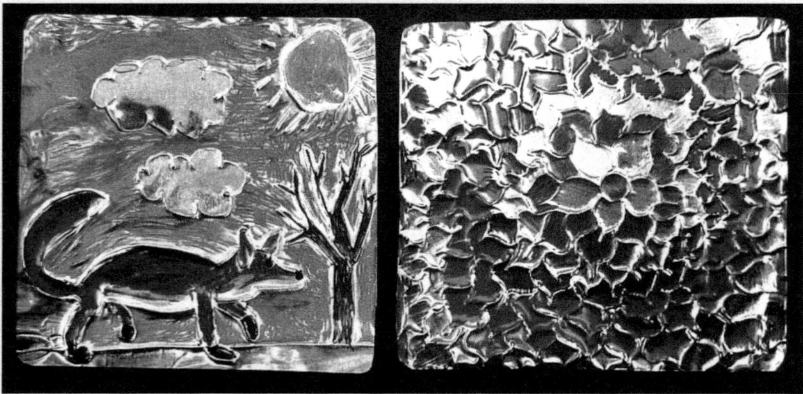

Figure 9.6   Artwork by Brian Dunham and Sarah Lancaster.

METAL TOOLING FOIL SHEETS

5" × 5" sheets of foil sheets—38 gauge, aluminum with copper coating on one side

Fine point (not ultrafine) permanent markers

6" × 6" (or larger) squares of craft felt

Wooden or plastic styluses (optional)

Preparation: With scissors, trim each piece of foil so that the edges are rounded and not sharp.

Cover the table with a plastic tablecloth with brown craft paper on top to protect surfaces.

Table Setup: Put one square of craft felt with a piece of foil on top for each person.

Place a stylus nearby.

Distribute various colors of permanent markers in bins down the center of the table.

Guidelines: Explain that this aluminum foil is an artist's material. It is thick enough to hold its shape and can be embossed with the stylus by making grooves in the foil.

The soft felt underneath will help make it easier to draw an impression into the foil.

Participants can choose to work on the copper-toned side and/or the silver-toned aluminum side.

Keep in mind that all impressions on the foil will be reversed on the opposite side.

The permanent markers will add color to the artwork. The permanent markers can also be used without the stylus to make impressions while coloring the foil.

Special Note: The permanent markers—especially the neon colors—have a luminous, translucent quality that is more vibrant on the silver-toned aluminum side.

Variations: Have a variety of precut sizes available. This will also allow for experimentation on smaller pieces before trying a larger size. Metal tooling foil sheets can also be used to make "illuminated initials" of the children's names based on medieval manuscript embellished lettering.

Rolls of metal foil (12in. × 25ft.) can also be purchased for larger projects, for example, creating art inspired by medieval shields. Prepare the shields beforehand by cutting out and gluing a two-inch cardboard frame to encase the edges of the metal and back it entirely with sturdy cardboard (not corrugated). Children can design their own protective dragon, or coat of arms, and design unique symbols on their shield.

ART FOR PEACE

Various colors of cardstock

12" × 18" drawing paper

Paint markers

Glue sticks

Scissors

Tape

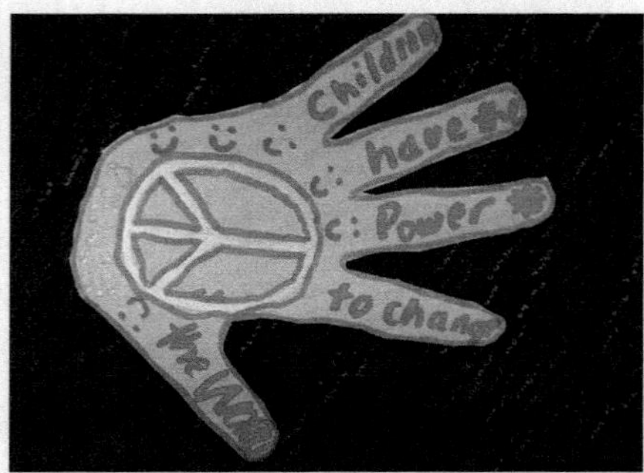

Figure 9.7 Detail of the Art for Peace mural. Photograph courtesy of the Avon Free Public Library.

Preparation: Cut cardstock in half.

Protect art table surface with plastic and brown craft paper.

Research art as a means of expression regarding social and environmental issues and causes, with examples of individual and collaborative artworks for peace.

Table Setup: Protect the table with a plastic tablecloth and brown craft paper.

Place a variety of colored cardstock and large (12" × 18") white paper in the center of the table.

Separated into bins, place a variety of paint markers, including white, silver, and gold, to be shared by participants.

Display examples of art for various causes from around the world.

Guidelines: Invite everyone to create a part of a collaborative effort for peace. Ask participants to create a poster and/or create a "hand for peace" with a message that will be displayed together as a mural.

Share the results with the group and discuss how art can make a difference in the world.

Note: The International Day of Peace (United Nations) is September 21.

Variations: Encourage children and teens to choose other issues and to express their beliefs and concerns through individual art statements and collaborative works.

Use hands as symbols for other collaborative themes, such as diversity.

PAINTING A MURAL IN A WORKSHOP BY HERVÉ TULLET

Children's book illustrator and author Hervé Tullet is world renowned for his numerous innovative and interactive children's books, including *Press Here* and *Mix It Up.* He is also known for *Art Workshops for Children,* a book describing group art experiences charged with energy and fun for all ages. According to Tullet, "I have developed my workshops guided by the idea that the art is a means and not an end. Children are masters of creation— they are very intuitive and it is this instinct and their unedited ability to create art that inspires me" (Tullet 2015, 5).

Tullet conducted a workshop for adults in 2015 at the Eric Carle Museum of Picture Book Art. Attended by some staff members of Avon

Free Public Library, it was an extraordinary chance to learn from Tullet's expertise and the experience is worth sharing with those who may never have a chance to meet him.

Tullet is a tall slender man with disheveled graying hair, paint-splotched jeans, and—surprisingly—bare feet. He gestured with the grace of a dancer and speaks with simple eloquence through a heavy French accent. With humor and humility, he described how his limited art abilities may have actually opened the way for his success in illustration. His playful approach to art aims to overcome fears and reduce inhibitions about creating skilled art products.

Tullet is an undeniable original. His enthusiasm is palpable. He is simultaneously prepared, spontaneous, and mischievously at play with his audience. His interactive children's books are brimming with whimsical silliness and fun. He read one of his newest books to us as if we were in storytime, leading us into a hilarious back-and-forth response.

Something about Tullet—what he is saying and how he is saying it—is an invitation for us all to let go just a little—and maybe even a little more. It is obvious that he is having fun. So should we. He then invited us to take part in a painting workshop to make a mural. It is intended for children. No, it is intended for the child in all of us. Tullet understands that the leader of such a workshop is a facilitator. He has compared the role to that of a musical conductor. But there is also something else. Like a jazz musician plays with sound, Tullet plays with art. What is more, everyone is invited to play along, no experience necessary. He invites collaborative work—that is actually no work at all—it is a performance, and everyone has a part. The session is utterly engaging and exciting, because no one is quite sure what will happen next.

Everyone has their own cup of paint and a brush, and there is a long roll of paper on the table. But our territory on the mural is not our own. Tullet has us move around the mural as if this was a game of musical chairs—except this is without the chairs—and no one is excluded by the game. Tullet tells us what is next: "Paint a dot." We all do. "Now change places and paint a bigger dot. . . " We all do. This goes on for a while as we move around the table. Then we hear, "Now make a circle!" We do, and then we swap places again and make bigger circles. Tullet observes that the mural is pretty, maybe it is *too* pretty. We are told to hold our paintbrushes high and then drop them on the mural! We do . . . and paint splatters! Then we move around again. He says, "Now we are going to transform these dots, circles and blotches into a field of flowers!"

Oh! Now we are making a wild garden! It grows fantastically in all directions! On the other side of the table, it is upside down. Or is it? Is it art? Who knows? It is fun. It is liberating. Art can be fun again without caring if it is right or wrong. This is the message. Those who never feel creative, suddenly feel creative. Those who are artists but have constricted their creativity to "art" will understand that it is more . . . much more. It is all on a continuum. This field of flowers mural is liberating for everyone. All the mistakes, splatters, and blotches are inspirations. We come to realize that his playful strategy is intentional, and it is deliberately designed to set us free.

Tullet chooses music to suit the mood he intends to create, at first to energize and then to calm. As the facilitator of the group, he establishes the rhythm and provides balance by moving around the mural to point out empty places that will lead away from overworked areas. Knowing when to stop is key.

"A Field of Flowers" mural and many other inspirational ideas and activities can be found in Hervé Tullet's delightful book *Art Workshops for Children*. Those who take part in these experiences create freely, knowing there is no right or wrong. When splotches can become inspirations, everyone can enjoy making art together!

Murals, art activities, and art games inspired by Tullet were later used for collaborative works during special events held in the Avon Free Public Library and for the "Book Buddies" program.

BOOK BUDDIES

The Book Buddies program at the Avon Free Public Library brings teens together with younger children to support literacy and creativity. Coordinated by Teen Librarian Marisa Hicking, 15 teen "big buddies" (grades 7–12) are each matched with "little buddies" (grades K-3). Before meeting the younger children for the first time, the teens are trained on verbal reading and listening skills, as well as how to talk with young children about their art.

The Book Buddies sessions take place once a week after school for about five weeks. Everyone meets collectively during the first part of the group. Then teens pair with their little buddies to read in various parts of the library. Afterward they all gather in the studio for a group art experience. These sessions avoid assembly-type crafts and offer choice-based art experiences. Everyone defines themselves as "artists." Often, the art ideas for the buddies were inspired by Open Art Studio, such as tissue collage. Simple art experiences everyone can do are chosen to bridge age differences and open up ways to connect with one another.

The collaborative art experiences in Hervé Tullet's book, *Art Workshops for Children*, have inspired many art experiences in the Book Buddies sessions. The Mural of Hands (Figure 9.8) was inspired by Tullet's "A Body of Work" (Tullet 2015, 46–49). Using the variation of painting overlapping hands, the resulting mural was as compelling for its artistry as it was for its eloquence as a metaphor for collaboration.

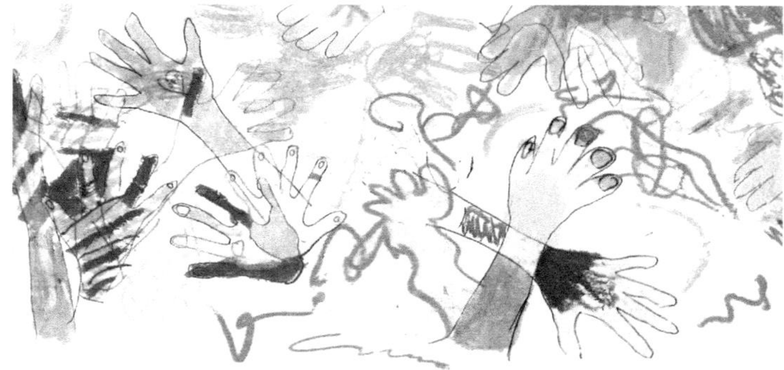

Figure 9.8   Mural of Hands. Photograph courtesy of the Avon Free Public Library.

Tullet's "A Field of Flowers" (8–13) was also a joy for the buddies to make together. The only disappointment was that the collaborative works could not go home with the children. Then the idea came to cut the large murals into small pieces that could be laminated later into bookmarks. At the end of the series of sessions, each big and little buddy was given a piece of their collaborative art to commemorate their time together, and nothing could be more fitting than an art bookmark to signify the connection between literacy and art.

TEENS IN OPEN ART AND ELSEWHERE

Teens who take part in the Open Art Studio program usually arrive with a small group of friends and tend to stay for quite a while. Art is a break from the after-school routine of homework, gaming, and social media. The pressure is off academically and socially at least for a while. No one grades or critiques their art in the library. Here teens can show off their art skills to an admiring younger audience or just join in a creative playtime. The inner child has a chance to emerge and have a little fun freely drawing, swishing paint, or forming clay.

Art making with teens does not need to be in an art room. Art materials can regularly be set up on a table in the teen area. This can be as simple as covering an entire tabletop with a large piece of brown craft paper and providing markers or colored pencils to draw and write on it. Many teens will have a chance to work on it over time. This artwork is expected to be temporary, and the paper will simply be replaced from time to time. There will be no up or down. No cohesive theme. Just a place for ideas. As time goes on, these works might give the impression of graffiti with stylized lettering, small drawings, and symbols to comment on social issues, convey moods, and express humor through this ephemeral collective art.

Providing folded cardstock with envelopes, markers, or colored pencils will entice teens to sit together and design their own cards. Handmade cards effortlessly enfold art into literacy and creative writing. Many teens have the expertise to make elaborate cards with calligraphy, pop-ups, and other ingenious methods. When given the chance, teens have gathered to make thoughtful "get well" cards to collectively send messages to classmates recovering from accidents or serious illnesses.

One Teen Advisory Board (TAB) meeting featured making bookmarks as gifts for a friend in recovery from a long illness. In another TAB meeting, bookmarks were made as random acts of kindness. With positive messages, quotes about literacy, and teen art doodles, teens hid the bookmarks in their favorite library books to be discovered later. Not every teen, however, will feel confident about art making, even on a space as small as a bookmark. To encourage giving art a try, offer a ruler. The teen librarian found that this was a most effective tool for teens who claim to have no skill or ideas. She encourages simply making lines. Just straight lines on the bookmarks resulted in strikingly intricate geometric designs.

Consider saving teen magazines for collage and decoupage. Teens appreciate recycling and repurposing discarded items into works of art. Book pages, maps, and sheet music can also be the inspiration for collage, decoupage, jewelry, folded art, origami, and so much more. Amazing ideas emerge when printed pages are used by teens as the background for art images, such as a portrait superimposed on a map.

Teens are at the ideal age to creatively use discarded book pages as a source for *found poetry*. Words on the page are selected and highlighted to create an original poem in this form of altered book art. Found poetry is known for both the expressive value of the poem and for the artistic use of negative space. Words chosen on the page are visually isolated and enclosed, while all other aspects of the page can be used for art design and imagery that can visually resonate the impact of the poem. For example, if the word "thunderstorm" was chosen along with other found words for a poem, this could be surrounded by dark swirls of clouds and lines of wind-driven rain. Art and literacy are thoroughly intertwined in found poetry.

Teens can also transform discarded CDs into imaginative and intricate works of art using sharpies or paint pens. With wire and string, these works collectively can become a dazzling CD mobile. CDs can also be glued artfully together for collaborative abstract wall art, or even a 3-D sculpture for the library. Or, with the insertion of inexpensive clock works, each CD can go home to become an iridescent art timepiece!

Because there does not need to be a separate art area, art materials can be delivered to tables where teens gather using an "open art cart" supplied and monitored by staff. Art supplies can change weekly or be cumulative by gradually adding more alternatives to what was previously offered, starting with basic drawing supplies, and then eventually including a selection of other materials for creating collages, painting, and working with clay. Although the art cart can be a "self-serve" area, this is not passive programming. A facilitator should be nearby at all times.

Art can be incorporated into many teen activities, such as book discussions and groups for homeschooled teens. Try tooling foil, mask making, illuminating initials, designing notebook covers, as well as illustrating and writing short stories. Invite teens to take part in making banners, signs, and flyers for upcoming events. Instead of clip art, use teen art to promote programs to make it authentically their own from the beginning.

If there is an art studio area, consider scheduling time just for teens to use the studio. A Teen Open Art Studio program could consist of a series of art experiences specifically designed by the creativity facilitator with the interests of teens in mind. Or, each session could offer a wide choice of art media arranged in separate areas of the room: centers for drawing, pastels, painting, collage, assemblage, and clay with the choice of medium selected by each teen.

Fundamentally, creativity facilitators open the way for group members to explore their own choices. Art materials and themes are selected to capture imaginations and then set them free. Open-ended ideas spark excitement and ignite an expansive array of creative reactions that radiate possibilities, freeing curious minds to venture beyond by lighting their own way.

10

Setup, Assessment, and Documentation

SETTING UP FOR ART

It is not necessary to have an art studio or even a separate room for art. There does not have to be a table or even a building. Creative art can be made with wet sand on a beach, chalk on the sidewalk, a stick in the dirt, or with the tip of a finger in the misty condensation of a window. Art can be done under the humblest of circumstances with the simplest of materials. If there is a will, there truly will be a way. If all you have is the basics, then that is all you need.

Art basics can be placed on a cart and taken anywhere. Just one folding table can become the art studio area. This table can be set up and taken down each time if space is at a premium. Just be sure it is adjusted to child level and set with child-size chairs. Chairs should be sturdy and wide enough for adults. These approximate measurements are a general guideline: chair seat height: 13 to 16 inches and table height: 21 to 24 inches.

If possible, have two tables: one main table 24 inches high, set with 16-inch chair seats, will be comfortable for most children and adults. Another lower table 21 inches high, set with 13-inch chair seats, will be more suitable for art making with younger children.

If possible, add an even lower table that is sized at the height of a coffee table, about 15 inches high or so. This will accommodate standing toddlers. Older children to adults can kneel or sit on the floor. This will be a great place for babies and toddlers to stand and scribble on large paper with toddler-size crayons. It will also be a compatible space for texture plate rubbing with large-size crayons. This area will attract people of all ages. Place a sign on this table: "Caregivers, Please Be Watchful at All Times."

Usually a library already has all the basics for art: paper, pencils, crayons, markers, scissors, tape, and glue. There may also be some brushes and liquid tempera paint. Already this is more than enough to do a series of creative art sessions. But libraries have much more. There is always plenty of cardboard for constructing and abundant discards: books, atlases, music books, magazines, newspapers, and old CDs. With a little string and small branches or sticks, there are the makings of mobiles. Save cardboard tubes from paper towel rolls for 3-D constructions or use the open cylinder ends as tools for circle paintings. Now there is the basis for an entirely different series of creative art experiences. No one has spent a penny on art supplies yet.

Facilitators can be creatively resourceful when the budget for art is extremely low. Begin by asking if any items could be used for art that are in the craft supply closet. It could be everything and it could be nothing. Always respect the rights of staff to keep materials designated for other purposes. Put in a request for any discards that might be thrown away. Neatly store these materials in a way that does not displace other items previously stored. Be careful not to intrude on anyone else's system of organization. Always ask permission to use anything, including equipment and storage space. Art-based creativity programs must not be seen as displacing or competing with other programs but rather as enhancing and expanding library offerings.

The care you take will be noted as a sign of respect. A new creative art program in a library will be evaluated according to many measures. Statistics of attendance are only one. Other staff members will notice if you are organized, on time, and respectful of shared spaces. Many may be dubious about whether creative art belongs in a library. As we all know, being creative often means being messy. So take extra care after every art session to thoroughly clean the art area. If someone later finds a counter full of drying cups to be stacked and put away in your absence, then you have impinged on their time and space. If a table has glue marks, and there are flecks of tissue on the floor, then all the more time will be spent setting it right. It is unfair to leave a room this way. Even small infractions can lead to justified resentment. The best policy is to leave no mark, to always return a room to exactly the way you found it. Yes, it is tedious to be so fastidious. Alas, someone has to do it!

THE GREAT CREATE

How can another library start up an art-based creativity program that is based on the Open Art Studio at the Avon Free Public Library? One illustrative example is *The Great Create* program that takes place in the adjacent town of Simsbury, Connecticut. Designed by Mary Fletcher in partnership with librarians April Jones and Chelesea Jenkins, the Simsbury and Avon programs have many similarities and some important differences. The duration of open time and frequency of the programs is not the same. The Great Create is scheduled once a month for one or two hours on a Sunday. The Open Art Studio has longer hours and takes place more frequently, typically four times a month on a weekday—usually Wednesdays—and is open from three to four hours on these days.

Two staff members facilitate The Great Create program, but due to staff scheduling limitations, only one can be present in the art room at a time. Duties are usually alternated between the reference/circulation desk and the art room. Fortunately, this area is near the desk. Much of the wall and doors are windowed to view between the two rooms.

As it is often the case in libraries, the area for art in Simsbury is a shared space. Known as the Children's Discovery and Science Center, the room is used for storytime, craft, and a variety of educational and entertainment programs. There is a floor-to-ceiling mural that wraps much of the room, depicting a marvelous panorama of the local landscape along with a group of reading children jauntily perched up on the branch of a sycamore tree. This mural certainly adds artistry to the space; but for art-making purposes, the area had several disadvantages from the start: the floor was recently carpeted, and the available folding tables and chairs for the room were sized for adults. Fortunately, the height of the tables could be adjusted lower and suitable chairs purchased for the room.

The many advantages of the room include a sink, a paper towel dispenser, a wall of storage cabinets, and sufficient space to fit several folding tables end to end and seat about 10–12 people. There is also space for an additional low table and four small chairs suitable for toddlers and younger children. This table and chairs are from the library play area and carried in for each art session. It is usually set simply with markers and paper to provide an alternative from the art experience on the main table. Since there are no drying racks for wet items, a plastic tarp is placed on the floor in a remote corner as a drying area for art. All in all, the room is easily made viable for open art making.

An art studio is primarily a concept and secondarily a place. Existing spaces do not have to be ideal for creating art. There will always be advantages and disadvantages in any location. With innovative thought, careful coordination, and a spirit of cooperation, the environment can be adapted to meet the needs of an art studio and continue to serve all other purposes as well.

This was an excellent way to learn about shared spaces. From the beginning, it became our priority to be mindful of others and to leave no trace. Tables were dutifully covered with protective plastic or paper, preferably both. After each art session, the room was returned to exactly the way it was found before it began. Floors were swept or vacuumed, sinks washed out, and everything put in its place. Sometimes volunteer help was available, but ultimately the cleanup responsibility belonged to the facilitator. When scheduling time for groups, the setup and cleanup time were easy to underestimate. It took much longer than realized, especially when painting materials, trays, and containers needed to be set out and then rinsed, dried, and carefully stored away. Brushes will require special diligence in cleansing and proper storage. But taking the time to clean supplies and organize shared spaces will always be essential for the continuance of any art program in a public building.

When The Great Create program first began several years ago, the storage cabinets mainly contained craft supplies. Much of this was usable for art: scissors, crayons, markers, glue, paper, tissue, and a few serviceable brushes. Nevertheless, there needed to be an investment in quality brushes, paints, watercolor paper, oil pastels, soft pastels, and clay. These and other art supplies were budgeted and funded over time. Many of these investments and others, such as trays, no-spill paint cups, and durable plastic table coverings have proven useful for other library programs too.

When the program first began, we were prepared for the initial reaction of the parents based on experience with an open art studio. As before, library patrons expected to drop their children off for craft time. But when asked to stay for art, caregivers came to appreciate having a chance to share this time with their children. Participants learned to accept the novel notion that there were no directions and that they were free to choose what to do. They could move freely around the room, even leave and come back again during the long session. Certain families began to come regularly and plan their weekends around visiting the library for these creativity groups. Many stayed for hours and became deeply involved in their art.

Usually about 35 people attend over a two-hour Sunday session and so the pace of The Great Create program has been relatively leisurely. It has a different pace than the Open Art Studio, which can have over 35 attendees an hour and well over a hundred participants over a three-hour period.

The Great Create program is rarely crowded, and the ambience is easygoing and calming. The music chosen enhances this tranquil and contemplative atmosphere. As a result, people tend to stay longer and invest in the process. Because these groups tend to be low key, this time has proven to be an "incubator" for trying out new ideas by experimenting with art materials and techniques. Blending oil pastel with baby oil was one such session. Using cotton swabs as the blender on cardstock, participants were fascinated by what happened when the oil pastel seemed to melt and turn into paint! Blending colors into one another resulted in velvety soft tints unachievable with oil pastel alone. Many chose to make abstract designs, florals, or landscapes that day. In the end, everyone laughed when a child exclaimed that room smelled good like babies!

In another session, white air-dry clay was offered that first met with a tentative response. But interest gradually began to build as little villages, trains, tiny rabbits, birds, and other marvels of imagination emerged from the clay. One father showed his artwork to his daughter, who gasped in amazement. "I didn't know you could make houses!" Soon she made a tiny house of her own and planted a tree in her yard. At the other end of the table, a girl made a white rainbow from concentric coils of clay, while a smaller boy nearby played with the clay by pinching it apart into small pieces. He saw the girl rolling the clay and gathered his clay bits and gave it a try. Soon he realized that he had shaped a snake and could make snake babies too!

Another child formed a little bunny that hopped around on the table. Nearby, a bird laid eggs and sat on her clay nest. An older boy made a slice of pepperoni pizza that got everyone talking about food. Someone had the idea to make a miniature birthday cake complete with a candle. Everyone sang "Happy Birthday." The families at this table had never met before but freely talked and laughed together and admired each other's work. These memorable shared experiences are infused with an exuberant spirit of joyful creative play.

The facilitator helps create this cheery atmosphere by inviting playfulness, knowing that play is at the core of creativity. Play makes the work of art no work at all. By taking the need to make a specific product literally off the table, no one is intimidated by the requirement to make a craft or art— or anything at else for that matter. When nothing needs to be anything, then things can happen. Then it is okay to be playful, be carefree, be optimistic, mess around, take chances, make mistakes, do something silly, and be totally spontaneous! When it is all right to have fun, and defenses go down, this is when ideas arise and amazing things happen.

As pediatrician and psychoanalyst D. W. Winnicott once said, "When we are surprised at ourselves, we are being creative, and we find we can trust our own unexpected originality" (Winnicott 1986, 51).

EQUIPMENT AND SPACE

What do libraries already have that can be used to supply a creative space? A booklet stapler (that has been used to repair magazines) will offer an efficient way to produce many small blank books at a relatively low cost. Does your library have a cutting machine, a laminator, a color printer? All are ideal for art making. Always keep cut scraps and remnants—everything around the cut shape—for collage. They are superb abstract shapes, often with brilliant coloration. Plastic laminator scraps are also well worth keeping. Save whatever would be thrown away. These scraps are sturdy and have a lovely translucent surface for art. Laminator scraps can be cut into geometric, free-form, or other shapes such as birds and detailed with permanent markers for mobiles.

Color printers create a lot of beautiful mistakes that just get recycled or tossed away. Request that these be set aside for future collages. Copiers and color printers are also an excellent way to collect and document artwork through printing digital photographs and making copies of art. This way children's work can be displayed without ever taking the original away from the artist.

Are there blank walls and windows in the library that can hold murals or become an art gallery? Always ask permission first, but these areas can be the ideal way to demonstrate and exhibit what is happening in art sessions. When mounting murals on walls, be careful to use adhesives that can be removed without damaging surfaces. On windows, liquid laundry starch can be applied to the glass so tissue paper will adhere for a temporary mural that will have a stained-glass effect when light penetrates (see City Collage). Taping paper artwork to glass can be done by curling tape first and placing it behind, so the art will be much easier to remove later. Avoid strong adhesives and double-sided tape. Temporary murals can be secured to walls in small sections using removable mounting putty. Expect that if the murals are to remain for a few months, they will need to be reattached in places from time to time.

SUPPLYING AN ART STUDIO

Below is a list of art supplies that will be useful to establish, sustain, and eventually enrich the possibilities of an art studio. Always check that materials are nontoxic before purchasing. Observe and follow any warnings about choking hazards, age restrictions, and safety recommendations for young children.

The initial investment in quality art supplies, containers, and tools can be expensive. Plan to buy over time as budget allows, starting with the basics. Whenever possible, buy in bulk, use coupons, and search for sales. Take the time for comparison shopping online with Amazon and various art, school, and discount supply sites, but do not settle for inferior quality just to save a little money. Low quality and cheap off-brand art materials usually perform poorly, frustrate and hinder artistry, and ultimately will not last. These are no bargain. Invest in higher value materials for durability and quality results. Research bargains on excellent brands. Local craft and office supply stores often have some unbeatable prices with coupons and sale items.

With careful use and maintenance, the majority of these art supplies will last for many sessions. Some will last for years, and others will never require replacement. They will yield results that are as incalculable as they are enduring. This is a quality investment in creativity.

BASIC SUPPLIES AND SUGGESTED MATERIALS

Basic and Useful Items: Children's safety scissors-blunt tip (also purchase scissors for left-handed children), transparent tape, masking tape, glue sticks, white glue, quick grab glue, mounting putty, liquid starch (tissue collage adhesive), string, stapler, hole punch, gallon plastic bags, paper plates (various sizes and colors), plastic table covers, and wet towelette wipes.

Paper: Inexpensive copy paper in various standard sizes: 8.5" × 11" and 11" × 17"
> Cardstock 8.5" × 11" White, black, dark blue, red, brights, and pastels
> Envelopes 6" × 9"
> White drawing paper 9" × 12"—500 Sheets
> Brown craft paper roll 36" × 1000' and paper holder with cutter 36" width (craft paper to be used for table coverings and murals)

Watercolor paper: 50- or 100-sheet bulk pack 12" × 18" 90#–135# (to be cut into 6" × 6" squares or larger)

Art tissue paper: All colors bleeding and nonbleeding and patterned tissue paper

Markers: Washable and non-washable markers (broad and fine line) in classpacks from school supply sources

Dot markers: Colorations Mini Dabber Dot Markers—set of 24

Paint: Nontoxic tempera paint block sets with trays, 6 assorted opaque blocks (also called tempera cakes) large 2 1/4" × 3/4" (10 sets)
> Liquid washable tempera: white, black, red, yellow, blue—gallons with pump dispensers

Paint brushes: Synthetic, sizes 8 to 12—round and flat quality brushes, with various other sizes and types

No-spill paint cups with translucent lids—3 1/2" high × 3" diameter—Pack of 10—(2 sets)

Paint markers: Water-based, medium, or fine point. Silver and gold—(3 sets) primary colors with black and white—(3 sets) or paint marker pens, medium point set of 15 (2 sets)

Trays: 12" × 16" black or dark color, set of 12 plastic trays (1 to 2 sets)

Oil pastels: Classpack (box of 336), 24 each of 10 colors, plus 48 each of black and white

Colored pencils: Bulk, 24 packs of 12 count

> Lyra Color Giants in assorted colors, set of 18
> Lyra Color Giants in skin tones, set of 12

Clay: Modeling compound in classpack: Primary colors (with white) or classpack white

> Air dry clay: white, nontoxic 25lb value pack

Clay modeling and sculpting tools: wooden or plastic (2 sets of various tools)

Nontoxic soft pastels: 3/4" × 2–1/2" size, assorted colors (pack of 48—two sets)

Texture plates: Various nature and pattern design texture rubbing plates

Crayons: Standard and large-size crayons (unwrapped)

> Triangular and other easy grip crayons for toddlers

Gel crayons or solid tempera paint sticks: Various colors and metallic

Woody 3 in 1 Colored Pencils: Set of 18 with sharpener (2 sets)

CREATIVE ART MATERIALS AND SPECIAL SURFACES

Permanent markers: 24 count fine tip in various colors. Neon in five colors (2 sets each)

Masks: White paperboard (paper mache) mask sets—6 per set—3 sets

Metal tooling foil sheets: Package of 12–5" × 5", 38 gauge or 12" × 25' roll

Frisbees: 9.5" nylon foldable flying discs with bags, white or light colors

Boxes: small lidded cardboard gift box sizes 3.75" × 3.75" × 3.4" black, white, and brown (craft store)

DISCARDS TO SAVE AND WHY

Paper and plastic scraps: Use discards from paper cutting and laminating for collage and mobiles

Discarded damaged books: Use picture and photography books for inspiration and reference. Use print books for altered books, word art, folded pages, and origami

Discarded CDs: Create art on CDs with permanent markers or paint markers. Paint with acrylic for "scratch art"

Puzzles with missing pieces: Use for 3-D art and assemblage

Maps and atlases: Make large paper airplanes, background art paper, and cut shapes for cards and collage

Magazines, music books, and old sheet music: Use for cards and collage

VALUATION THROUGH COMMUNICATION

As creativity facilitators we will be constantly evaluating our approach. This continuous assessment is the way to refresh our procedures while maintaining our own creativity. If a program is to be viable and sustainable, it must spiral back to those methods and materials that are fundamentally valuable and worth recreating while deliberately evolving outward over time.

Those who co-facilitate are in full partnership. Open communication is essential to assess programs in order to plan for the future. Materials need to be inventoried, budgets calculated, and sessions evaluated for effectiveness before plans can be designed. Arranged meetings should take place frequently, but the conversation should be ongoing. Some of the best ideas are exchanged when setting up before programs or cleaning up afterward. Sharing this time with a co-facilitator will be time well spent. This is the chance to privately discuss the day. It can bring closure to a busy session and provide a mental reset for next time.

After every session, assess what just happened. Were there any pleasant surprises? Any unexpected setbacks? What can be done differently next time? What merits repeating? Were there ideas or suggestions from participants? Were there some amusing moments? Remarkable happenings? What was the most memorable aspect of the day? What can we learn from all this? Reviewing the session will be key. Sharing different perspectives and methods of approach will lend fresh insights. Taking time to openly share opinions, perhaps disagree, listen respectfully, and work through challenges together needs to happen continuously.

Co-facilitators understand that drop-in programs are in flux and changeable—they need revision and redesign in order to consciously evolve. Adjustments will be made, for instance, when the majority of children attending the sessions are much younger or older than expected. Planning ahead is necessary, but plan too far ahead and flexibility might be sacrificed. For this reason, it may be advantageous not to advertise beforehand with specific information about art sessions to come. Then if a group requests a painting session soon, this can be planned without upsetting a prescheduled event.

Keeping official statistics of attendance for each session includes noting the number of adults, teens, and the number and approximate ages of children. In addition, each facilitator can also keep process notes on general observations. These notes can be kept for future reference and will assist in documenting, evaluating, and planning future sessions, as well as for presentations. Note what went well and what could be improved based on the reaction of the participants and list possible variations of the session based on these findings.

Much can be learned through ongoing study of creativity research and practice, as well as though learning from our own experiences. Documentation provides a way to visually reflect upon these experiences. Statistics only go so far. They cannot define the value of the experience for those who took part in it. Some of the most notable creativity sessions may have low attendance or happen during the "slow" time of a day. And so, documentation is not just about measuring numbers. It is about evaluating the value of the art experience for creativity. Was the experience of quality? Was the response enthusiastic? Was the process engaging? Was the resulting artwork rich in diversity? Did someone do something they never thought they could do before? Did someone say, "I never knew I was creative!"

DOCUMENTATION: PHOTOGRAPHING PROCESS AND ART

Photographs in the art studio hold moments in time that illustrate so much more. A baby makes her first tentative marks on paper while still being held in her mother's arms. A toddler gazes intently at the tip of his paintbrush that just made a long thin black line. A boy scribbles energetically across a wide swath of paper. A tiny hand is printed with blue paint. A young girl holds up her drawing as her grandmother glows with admiration. Small hands fasten the wings on a clay butterfly. A child bent intently over his artwork holds a pastel in a hand moving so quickly across the surface that it becomes a blur in the photograph. A girl hesitates before gluing a paper fragment, carefully considering where it belongs on her collage. A teen patiently renders intricate silver designs on black paper. Three generations of a family, each absorbed in their own painting, sit close by one another.

Photographing these moments will capture more than just the artwork. These are *people* being creative. This is the true heart of the art experience. Documenting artwork is necessary, but the process of making the art is at the center of creativity. It is the *work* of artwork. Many of these process photos reveal the intensity of involvement and deep engagement in decision making and problem solving. There may be a few photos that capture an "Aha!" moment, as an idea strikes and lights up a face with awe and inspiration, but usually the smiles shine with satisfaction while displaying the outcome of work well done.

Very young children often insist on being photographed holding their artwork with ecstatic grins on their faces. They also want to make sure that photographs have been taken of *all* their work. Older children and teens may not really want to be in the picture, but they are certainly pleased that their work is being photographed. Some offer to become involved in setting up their artwork for photography, and delight in posing clay figures of animals or staging a story scene. This is an extension of their creative process. Respect this by taking the time to allow the artist to arrange everything for the camera's eye before taking the final photographs. Take a series of photos from the angles they prefer. If time allows, lend the camera to each group member so they can be involved in photographing their own artwork.

Remember to always ask permission before taking a photograph, especially while a group is in process. Even with previous written consent to be photographed, it is courteous to ask. Sometimes children prefer not to have a photograph taken of work in progress, insisting that it is not finished yet. This is absolutely their right. Let them know this is fine. Move on and revisit later when the artwork is complete.

Be mindful to not intrude on the creative process. Never use a flash. Try not to hover or linger long in any one place. Be quick and efficient. Be as fair and even-handed as possible and sensitive to everyone's needs. It is a good policy to keep the camera away most of the time and only use it periodically for documentation. The professional appearance of a camera is preferable to a phone. Strictly speaking, a digital camera is a screen in a screen-free zone and tech in a tech-free zone. Of course, the use of a camera is always the exception for everyone in the art room. It is not a distraction from the art. The camera is literally focusing on the art and the art process. Photography is creative art. Technology that serves creative purposes belongs in art studios.

To take photography one step further, everyone can get involved in making a video of an art session. After all the necessary permissions are signed, have fun recording the creation of a mural or another interactive group art experience. Perhaps older children and teens could get involved by editing, adding music, and some special effects, so this documentary video also becomes a work of art!

Files of digital photos and videos, as well as the signed permission forms to use photos and videos will need to be kept well organized and accessible for future use. Back them up for safety to protect this data. Keep the permissions and releases in confidential files. Make sure that these documents specify the ways that the photographs may be used to promote the program and if they will be published online.

Photographs and documenting videos will be an ever expanding resource that can attest to the genuine scope of the program. It will be impressive for all to see the outcome of so much creative effort over time. This photographic archive will become the most authentic and enduring illustration of the value of art-based creativity programs in libraries.

With permission, images taken in the art studio can be posted on a library blog, included in presentations, and printed for a gallery display to educate about creativity programs. An ongoing art-related library blog featuring what has happened in the art studio along with upcoming events will heighten interest and enthusiasm. A blog that reaches outside and brings in the public will also reach inside to inform other library staff members about what has been going on. It will be worthwhile to also offer a workshop for staff, explaining much more than can be posted on a blog. A presentation that includes photos of the artists of all ages involved in the process would best illustrate the philosophy and approach of the creativity program. This could be augmented by offering an experiential component for the staff of a choice-based art experience followed by a discussion.

Images from library art events and activities will be indispensable for education, publicity, and ultimately keep creativity programs going. Art photos enhance flyers, enliven informational pamphlets, and attract attention to the posting of future events. Above all, these images honor the art process by documenting what has been accomplished.

Establish a library creative art gallery that displays the printed photographs of art made in the studio, so the actual artwork can always go home with the artist. This is especially important with young children, who are reluctant to give up their work even for display. Any empty wall can be transformed into a gallery wall but is best to choose a central area with good lighting where people tend to gather. Avoid strong direct sunlight that can fade photos and artwork over time. Trifold board displays can be used that are easily transported for presentations. Large 48" × 36" premium foam boards in black are a freestanding place for a creative arrangement of artwork photos. Use double-sided tape that is repositionable to mount the paper on the boards.

Every passerby to the art gallery will understand that these are photos of art being made in the library, ranging from scribbles to sculptures, from splashes of paint to scenic landscapes, from clay eggs to winged dragons. Periodically, the photos in the gallery exhibit can feature an entirely new display of ideas. Why not have informal art receptions to celebrate new art openings or murals? Simple refreshments can be served and the ambience enhanced with music. The family, friends, and everyone passing by will have a chance to celebrate the artists' work on the library wall.

ART DAY IN MAY

Art Day in May (or any other month) can become an annual event or be extended into series of special events throughout the year. These days serve to document the library's creativity programming and also to celebrate the arts in the community through dance, drama, and musical performances. The library becomes a place where local artists and artisans demonstrate their work; local authors give readings, and illustrators and writers of children's books offer storytime. Art Day invites public participation in creative movement, dance parties, drum circles, singing, and a chance to play along with simple musical instruments.

These days can offer a choice of creative experiences for all ages in the art studio and throughout the library. Supervised areas can be set up with clay, collage, and pastels. Simple blank books can be placed with various art supplies beckoning patrons to illustrate and write an original short story.

A spectacular collaborative mural can be completed by the public in a single day, such as the City Collage window mural. The Fish in the Sea mural began on an Art Day. Also, several different collaborative murals inspired by Hervé Tullet's art workshop ideas were made on these occasions.

These are just a few of the possibilities for Art Day. Of course, not everything can happen at once, but many of these events could occur simultaneously. Days such as these can also celebrate the outcome of a series of creativity sessions. An art reception with refreshments near an art display, mural, or gallery exhibit could run concurrently with all the other arts-related events in the library.

PRESENTATIONS

Once an arts-based creativity program is offered, others will want to know about it. Initially, word of mouth will promote the program. Library patrons delighted by the experience will tell friends. A following of faithful attendees will attract others. Soon the room will be filled to capacity. Local community papers will want to feature the program and more people will come in response. When a program is done well, it will be well attended.

When staff from other libraries express interest, this is the chance to spread the word. Accept requests to observe the program, and advocate for creativity in other libraries by reaching out through consultations and presentations.

The documentation of statistics, progress notes, and photographs will be a vast resource for presenting at conferences. Bring in everyone involved in creativity programming at the library to collaborate on a presentation. A presentation on creativity should be innovative, not just a litany of quotes and conclusions recited by the presenter. Of course, it will be essential to present research that validates the need for creativity programming in libraries, but go beyond this. Show videos of the art process, and let the audience hear and see the enthusiasm of the participants. Show the thrilled faces of the artists. Capture the fun. Put lively music behind the photos of the art at the end of the presentation. Make it a joy to be in the audience!

Afterword

BEYOND THE CREATIVE EDGE

Thoreau's thoughts about the inspiration of books can now be revisited; what you have begun by reading, it is hoped you will "finish by acting." Be inspired to use these ideas—and your own—to nurture creativity within yourself and others.

Beyond a doubt, creative and innovative minds will have a decided advantage in the future—the creative edge. Going beyond the individual, if libraries are to survive into the 22nd century, they must become creative, too. To navigate rapid changes and to successfully surmount escalating challenges, creativity will be a survival skill in the future—as it always has been in the past—for human beings throughout time. This is how we have come so far.

Children need creative resources. Beyond information, they also need inspiration. Libraries can be a source for this and heighten awareness that there needs to be a balance and a synergy between technology and creativity. Libraries can be centers for creativity and innovation. Perhaps the paradigm shifting libraries of the future will be designed with art studios and becoming a "library creativity specialist" will be a career choice. For now, changes such as these can be envisioned on the creative edge. We are on the verge.

***

The creative edge is a vantage point where it is possible to envision past the horizon. It is where vast distances become undeniably connected and boundaries dissipate. It is being here now—and always and anywhere.

165

Blink and it is a thousand years ago, blink again and it is a thousand years from now. Step up to the edge . . . and step once more . . . where to now?

> Smaller than an electron, it contains uncountable galaxies.
>
> —Lao Tzu, *Tao Te Ching,* Chapter 32 (translated into modern terms)

Take an imaginative leap from the edge of this precipice. It becomes startlingly clear that the sky is no longer the limit . . . the stars are within reach. Possibilities are vast, and unsolvable problems may have just not found their solutions yet. See by peering into darkness, understand by listening to silences. The infinite is in the infinitesimal.

Give form to what has never been before, shape imaginings, sing for the voiceless, and dance for joy . . . *create life as a work of art.*

Bibliography

Adams, Scott. 1996. *The Dilbert Principle*. New York: Harper Business.

Barnett, Meredith. 2013. "The Arts as a Bridge to Literacy: Arts-centric Instruction Can Bolster Student Reading and Writing." https://www.naesp.org/principal-supplement-septoct-2013-champion-creatively-alive-children/arts-bridge-literacy (Accessed July 7, 2018).

Bilton, Nick. 2014. "Steve Jobs Was a Low-Tech Parent." *New York Times*, September 10, 2014. /2014/09/11/fashion/steve-jobs-apple-was-a-low-tech-parent.html (Accessed December 5, 2018).

Bronson, Po and Ashley Merryman. 2009. *NurtureShock: New Thinking about Children*. New York: Hachette.

Cameron, Julia and Emma Lively. 2013. *The Artist's Way for Parents: Raising Creative Children*. New York: Penguin.

Carey, Ann, Ana Dziengel, Amber Scardino, Chelsey Marashian, Dayna Abraham, Erica Clark, Jamie Hand, Karyn Tripp, Leslie Manlapig, Malia Hollowell, and P. R. Newton. 2016. *STEAM Kids: 50+Science/Technology/Engineering/Art/Math Hands-On Projects for Kids*. STEAMkids@leftbraincraftbrain.com.

Clarke, Michael. 2010. *The Concise Oxford Dictionary of Art Terms*. New York: University Press.

Coyne, Sarah M., Jenny Radesky, Kevin M. Collier, Douglas A. Gentile, Jennifer Ruh Linder, Amy I. Nathanson, Eric E. Rasmussen, Stephanie M. Reich, and Jean Rogers. 2017. "Parenting and Digital Media." http://pediatrics.aappublications.org/content/140/Supplement_2/S112 (Accessed July 15, 2018).

Crayola. n.d. "CreatED: Professional Learning by Crayola." http://www.crayola.com/education/compelling.aspx (Accessed July 15, 2018).

Csikszentmihalyi, Mihaly. 1990. *Flow: The Psychology of Optimal Experience*. New York: Harper and Row.

Csikszentmihalyi, Mihaly. 1996. *Creativity: Flow and the Psychology of Discovery and Invention.* New York: HarperCollins.

Damon-Moore, Laura and Erinn Batykefer. 2014. *The Artist's Library: A Field Guide from the Library as Incubator Project.* Minneapolis, MN: Coffee House Press.

Danko-McGhee, Kathy and Ruslan Slutsky. 2007. *The Impact of Early Art Experiences on Literacy Development.* Reston, VA: National Art Association.

Douglas, Katherine M. and Diane B. Jaquith. 2009. *Engaging Learners Through Artmaking: Choice-Based Art Education in the Classroom.* New York: Teachers College Press.

Dweck, Carol S. 2006. *Mindset: The New Psychology of Success.* New York: Random House.

Edwards, Carolyn, Lella Gandini, and George Forman. 1993. "Introduction." In *The Hundred Languages of Children*, edited by Carolyn Edwards, Lella Gandini, and George Forman, 3–18. Norwood, NJ: Ablex.

Eric Carle Museum of Picture Book Art. 2018. "Our Approach." https://www.carlemuseum.org/content/our-approach (Accessed July 8, 2018).

Fleming, Amy. 2015. "Screen Time v Play Time: What Tech Leaders Won't Let Their Own Kids Do." https://www.theguardian.com/technology/2015/may/23/screen-time-v-play-time-what-tech-leaders-wont-let-their-own-kids-do (Accessed July 21, 2018).

Fletcher, Mary. 2016. "On the Creative Edge: The Artistic Side of One Library." *Children and Libraries: The Journal of the Association for Library Service to Children* 14(4): 10–12.

Gandini, Lella. 2015. "The Amusement Park for Birds: Emergence and Process of a Project." In *In the Spirit of the Studio: Learning from the Atelier of Reggio Emilia*, edited by Lella Gandini, Lynn Hill, Louise Cadwell, and Charles Schwall, 23–41. New York: Teacher's College Press.

Gardner, Howard. 1980. *Artful Scribbles: The Significance of Children's Drawings.* New York: Perseus Books.

Gardner, Howard. 1993. *Creating Minds: An Anatomy of Creativity Seen through the Lives of Freud, Einstein, Picasso, Stravinsky, Eliot, Graham, and Gandhi.* New York: Basic Books.

Gardner, Howard. 1993. "Foreword." In *The Hundred Languages of Children*, edited by Carolyn Edwards, Lella Gandini, and George Forman, ix–xiii. Norwood, NJ: Ablex Publishing.

Gardner, Howard. 1999. *Intelligence Reframed: Multiple Intelligences for the 21st Century.* New York: Basic Books.

Greenfield, Susan. 2015. *Mind Change: How Digital Technologies Are Leaving Their Mark on Our Brains.* New York: Random House.

Hadani, Helen, and Garrett Jaeger. 2015. *Inspiring a Generation to Create: Critical Components of Creativity in Children.* Sausalito, CA: CCC.

Hathaway, Nan E. 2012. "Outlaws, Rebels, and Rogues: Creative Under-achievers." In *The Learner-Directed Classroom: Developing Creative Thinking Skills Through Art,* edited by Diane B. Jaquith and Nan E. Hathaway, 79–89. New York: Teacher's College Press.

Henri, Robert. 2007. *The Art Spirit: Notes, Articles, Fragments of Letters and Talks to Students, Bearing on the Concept and Technique of Picture Making, the Study of Art Generally, and on Appreciation.* New York: Basic Books.

Jaquith, Diane B. and Nan E. Hathaway, Eds. 2012. *The Learner-Directed Classroom: Developing Creative Thinking Skills Through Art.* New York: Teacher's College Press.

Jobs, Steve. 2011. "Smithsonian Institution, Oral and Video Histories, April 20, 1995." In *I, Steve: Steve Jobs in His Own Words,* edited by George Beahm, 55. Chicago: B2 Books, Agate Imprint.

J. W. Killam School. 2015. "Killam Family Tree." killamcreationstation.blogspot.com/2015/02/killam-family-tree.html (Accessed May 25, 2015).

Kaufman, Scott and Carolyn Gregoire. 2015. *Wired to Create: Unraveling the Mysteries of the Creative Mind.* New York: Random House.

Kelley, Tom and Jonathan Littman. 2001. *The Art of Innovation: Lessons in Creativity from IDEO America's Leading Design Firm.* New York: Random House.

Kellogg, Rhoda. 2015. *Analyzing Children's Art.* Philadelphia, PA: Girard and Stewart.

Kiefer, Barbara Z. 1995. *The Potential of Picturebooks: From Visual Literacy to Aesthetic Understanding.* Englewood Cliffs, NJ: Prentice Hall.

Kohl, MaryAnn. 1994. *Preschool Art: It's the Process Not the Product.* Beltsville, MD: Gryphon House.

Krysa, Danille. 2014. *Creative Block: Advice and Projects from 50 Successful Artists.* San Francisco: Chronicle.

Lambert, Megan Dowd. 2015. *Reading Picture Books with Children: How to Shake Up Storytime and Get Kids Talking about What They See.* Watertown, MA: Charlesbridge.

Lehrer, Jonah. 2012. *Imagine: How Creativity Works.* New York: Houghton Mifflin Harcourt.

Longmore, Tannis. 2012. "Supporting Young Artists as Independent Creators." In *The Learner-Directed Classroom: Developing Creative Thinking Skills Through Art,* edited by Diane B. Jaquith and Nan E. Hathaway, 56–63. New York: Teacher's College Press.

Louv, Richard. 2005. *The Last Child in the Woods: Saving Our Children from Nature-Deficit Disorder.* New York: Algonquin.

MacKenzie, Diana. 2014. "A Place to Call Home." https://www.carlemuseum.org/blogs/making-art/archive/201405 (Accessed July 21, 2018).

Malaguzzi, Loris. 1993. "History, Ideas, and Basic Philosophy." In *The Hundred Languages of Children*, edited by Carolyn Edwards, Lella Gandini, and George Forman, 41–89. Norwood, NJ: Ablex Publishing.

Maslow, A. H. 1993. *The Farther Reaches of Human Nature*. New York: Penguin.

Matros, Bridget. 2010. "Handprint Turkeys and the Cotton Ball Snowman: Is There Hope for an Artful America?" In *20under40: Reinventing the Arts and Arts Education for the 21st Century*, edited by Edward P. Clapp, 310–330. Bloomingdale: AuthorHouse.

Matthews, Dona and Joanne Foster. 2014. *Beyond Intelligence: Secrets for Raising Happily Productive Kids*. Toronto: Anansi Press.

May, Rollo. 1975. *The Courage to Create*. New York: Norton and Company.

Mueller, Jennifer. 2017. *Creative Change: Why We Resist It . . . How We Can Embrace It*. New York: Houghton Mifflin Harcourt.

NAEYC/IRA. 1998. "Learning to Read and Write: Developmentally Appropriate Practices for Young Children." https://www.naeyc.org/sites/files/globally-shared/downloads/PDFs/resources/position-statements/PSREAD98.PDF (Accessed May 30, 2018).

New York Public Library. 2018. "Early Literacy in the New York Public Library." https://www.nypl.org/education/parents/early-literacy (Accessed May 11, 2018).

Nicoll, Meg. 2017. "Collaborative Window Collage." https://www.carlemuseum.org/blogs/making-art/collaborative-window-collage (Accessed January 11, 2019).

Olshansky, Beth. 2008. *The Power of Pictures: Creating Pathways to Literacy Through Art*. San Francisco: Jossey-Bass.

Pink, Daniel H. 2005. *A Whole New Mind: Moving from the Information Age to the Conceptual Age*. New York: Penguin.

Postman, Neil. 1994. *The Disappearance of Childhood*. New York: Random House.

Radesky, Jenny and Dimitri Christakis. 2016. "Media and Young Minds." http://pediatrics.aappublications.org/content/early/2016/10/19/peds.2016-2591 (Accessed July 15, 2018).

Richards, Ruth. 1996. "Beyond Piaget: Accepting Divergent, Chaotic, and Creative Thought." In *Creativity from Childhood Through Adulthood: The Developmental Issues*, edited by Mark A. Runco. *New Directions for Child Development* 72: 67–86.

Richards, Ruth. 2017. *Everyday Creativity: Coping and Thriving in the 21st Century*. Morrisville, NC: lulu.com.

Rinaldi, Carla. 2015. "The Whole School as Atelier: Reflections by Carla Rinaldi." In *In the Spirit of the Studio: Learning from the Atelier of Reggio Emilia*, edited by Lella Gandini, 43–47. New York: Teacher's College Press.

Robinson, Ken and Lou Aronica. *Creative Schools: The Grassroots Revolution That's Transforming Education*. New York: Viking, 2015.

Runco, Mark A. 1996. "Creativity and Development: Recommendations." In *Creativity from Childhood Through Adulthood: The Developmental Issues. New Directions for Child Development*, 72: 87–90.

Schoorel, Edmond. 2016. *Managing Screen Time: Raising Balanced Children in the Digital Age* (translated by Eduard van der Maas). Edinburgh: Floris Books.

Schwall, Charles. 2015. "Design Invent Play: Engaging Contemporary Culture." In *In the Spirit of the Studio: Learning from the Atelier of Reggio Emilia*, edited by Lella Gandini, Lynn Hill, Louise Cadwell, and Charles Schwall, 165–170. New York: Teacher's College Press.

Seelig, Tina. 2012. *inGenius: A Crash Course on Creativity*. New York: HarperCollins.

Sousa, David A. and Tom Pilecki. 2013. *From STEM to STEAM: Using Brain-Compatible Strategies to Integrate the* Arts. Thousand Oaks, CA: Sage Publications.

Steiner-Adair, Catherine and Teresa H. Barker. 2014. *The Big Disconnect: Protecting Childhood and Family Relationships in the Digital Age*. New York: HarperCollins.

Sterman, Cheri. 2017. "Collaborate Beyond School: Engage with Your Community." http://www.nxtbook.com/ygsreprints/NAESP/principal_crayolasupp_20170910 (Accessed July 15, 2018).

Sternberg, Robert J. 1996. *Successful Intelligence: How Practical and Creative Intelligence Determine Success in Life*. New York: Simon & Schuster.

Sternberg, Robert J. 2003. "The Development of Creativity as a Decision-Making Process." In *Creativity and Development*, edited by R. Keith Sawyer, Vera John-Steiner, Seana Moran, Robert J. Sternberg, David Henry Feldman, Jeanne Nakamura, and Mihaly Csikzentmihalyi, 91–138. New York: Oxford University Press.

Striker, Susan. 1986. *Please Touch: How to Stimulate Your Child's Creative Development through Movement, Music, Art and Play*. New York: Simon & Schuster.

Striker, Susan. 2001. *Young at Art: Teaching Toddlers Self-Expression, Problem-Solving Skills, and an Appreciation for Art*. New York: Henry Holt.

Taylor, Brandon. 2004. *Collage: The Making of Modern Art*. New York: Thames & Hudson.

Thoreau, Henry David. 1971. *Thoreau's World: Miniatures from His Journal*, edited by Charles R. Anderson. Englewood Cliffs, NJ: Prentice-Hall, Inc.

Thoreau, Henry David. 1980. *A Week on the Concord and Merrimack Rivers*, edited by Carle F. Hovde. Princeton, NJ: Princeton University Press.

Tullet, Hervé. 2015. *Art Workshops for Children*. London: Phaidon Press.

Tzu, Lao. 1999. *Tao Te Ching: An Illustrated Journey* (Translated by Stephen Mitchell). London: Frances Lincoln.

Viereck, George. 1929. "What Life Means to Einstein: An Interview by George Sylvester Viereck." *Saturday Evening Post* (October 26, 1929): 117.

Weiner, Robert Paul. 2000. *Creativity and Beyond: Cultures, Values and Change*. Albany, NY: State University of New York Press.

Weller, Chris. 2017. "Bill Gates and Steve Jobs Raised Their Kids Tech-Free—and It Should've Been a Red Flag." http://www.businessin sider.com/screen-time-limits-bill-gates-steve-jobs-red-flag -2017–10 (Accessed July 21, 2018).

Winnicott, D. W. 1986. "Living Creatively." In *Home Is Where We Start From: Essays by a Psychoanalyst*, edited by Clare Winnicott, Ray Shepard, and Madeleine Davis, 39–54. New York: W.W. Norton.

Yenawine, Philip. 2018. *Visual Thinking Strategies for Preschool: Using Art to Enhance Literacy and Social Skills*. Cambridge, MA: Harvard Education Press.

Index

About the Author

Mary C. Fletcher is an artist and illustrator, with a master of arts in art therapy. She is the Library Creativity Specialist at the Avon Free Public Library in Avon, Connecticut, which has established one of the first art studios located in a public library. The Avon Free Public Library was among the recipients awarded the ALSC Curiosity Creates grant funded by Disney. Mary's article "The Creative Edge: The Artistic Side of One Library" was published in the Winter 2016 edition of *Children and Libraries: The Journal of the Association for Library Service to Children.* The library's exemplary creativity programming was presented at The Symposium on the Future of Libraries in 2017.